D1427619

FORD PICKUP TRUCKS

Mike Mueller

m motorbooks

First published in 2008 by Motorbooks, an imprint of MBI Publishing Company, 400 First Avenue North, Suite 300, Minneapolis, MN 55401 USA

The information in this book is true and complete to the best of our knowledge. All recommendations are made without any guarantee on the part of the author or Publisher, who also disclaim any liability incurred in connection with the use of this data or specific details.

This publication has not been prepared, approved, or licensed by Ford Motor Company.

We recognize, further, that some words, model names, and designations mentioned herein are the property of the trademark holder. We use them for identification purposes only. This is not an official publication.

Motorbooks titles are also available at discounts in bulk quantity for industrial or sales-promotional use. For details write to Special Sales Manager at MBI Publishing Company, 400 First Avenue North, Suite 300, Minneapolis, MN 55401 USA.

To find out more about our books, join us online at www.motorbooks.com.

ISBN-13: 978-0-7603-3262-7

Editor: Peter Schletty
Designer: Jennifer Maass

Printed in China

Contents

Over the Long Haul

Introduction

Ford's latest, greatest F-150 is not only America's best-selling truck, it's also the longest running, tracing its roots back to Dearborn's original F-series pickup, introduced for 1948. This F-1 model, in turn, appeared some 30 years after Henry Ford had rolled out his very first truck, the Model TT one-ton, in July 1917. Sold only in bare-chassis form early on, the burly, bare-bones TT at the time was certainly nothing new on the utility vehicle scene. But it did represent a major milestone as far as today's ongoing Big Three truck legacy is concerned—it got the ball rolling. Dodge's first civilian-market commercial vehicle (the company had begun building military-use-only trucks in 1916) followed Ford's in October 1917, and Chevrolet's first debuted in January 1918.

Ford again made truck history eight years later by introducing America to the modern pickup. Sure, light-duty half-ton trucks had existed before 1925, but not one was factory built. Aftermarket companies supplied custom pickup bodies up to that point, and nearly all of these were made rather crudely of wood. Ford's 1925 Model T Runabout with Pick-Up Body broke ground because it was sold complete from Dearborn with a steel body. No more middleman suppliers, and no more open invitations to termites.

Though another factory-built pickup, this one from Dodge Brothers, had actually debuted the year before, it apparently failed to qualify for milestone status due to various technicalities. This 3/4-ton truck featured an archaic wooden body supplied by the Graham Brothers firm, Dodge's Indiana-based "truck division." Additionally, it was barely noticed by truck buyers—only about 500 were built in 1924, compared to the 30,000 Model T pick-ups delivered by Ford in 1925.

By 1930, both Chevrolet and Dodge had cut out the middleman (as well as the carpenter) by rolling out their own steel-bodied pickups, signaling the end of an era. Quaint wooden truck cabs would remain on the scene a bit longer, but the various companies that once fashioned them by the boatload quickly faded away.

Ford kicked off the Big Three truck race in 1917, introducing its Model TT one-ton, sold initially only in bare-chassis form. The TT then was followed eight years later by America's first factory-complete, steel-bodied pickup. To the right of the 1925 Model T truck here is a 1926 Model TT.

Competitive juices, meanwhile, began boiling as Ford and Chevy kept busy battling for the truck market sales lead. Upstart Chevrolet first took the top spot from the reigning champ in 1927, and the two battled back and forth through the Thirties. Chevrolet regained the number one position in 1938 and stayed in front for another 30 years. Now it's Ford with the bragging rights of 30 straight years building America's most popular pickup.

While Chevrolet trucks stayed out in front during the first two decades following World War II, Ford's counterparts in those days were by no means also-rans. Dearborn's first new postwar pickup, the aforementioned F-1, was followed five years later by a true American milestone. When *Automobile* magazine named "The 24 Most Important Automobiles of the Century" in its September 1996 issue, included along with the likes of Ford's first Model T was the 1953 F-100. "Every comfortable, driver-friendly pickup on the road today owes its existence to the original Ford F-100," wrote *Automobile* founder

Ford was still simply modifying its cars into light-duty pickups as the Thirties dawned. Behind the 1929 pickup here is a 1928 Model A coupe (left) and a 1930 Tudor (right), all demonstrating those family ties.

What a difference 35 years can make: the F-100 on the left was still very much a truck in 1956, while the 1991 F-150 on the right—even in rugged 4x4 form—was almost as much at home downtown as it was off road.

David E. Davis, Jr. "Until the appearance of the restyled F-100 pickup, trucks were thought suitable only for commercial uses. But [this] was the first truck planned, styled, and engineered by a corporate management team, and suddenly pickups became an alternative for personal transportation."

Although it, too, failed to immediately bring down the Bow-Tie, the F-100 remained hot on the leader's heels year in and year out until the job was finally done. After returning to the top in 1968, the F-100 was joined by its F-150 heavy half-ton running mate seven years later. The F-150 then supplanted the F-100 as

Ford's 2007 Super Duty King Ranch is truly representative of just how much the car and truck worlds have merged in recent years. This big baby is amazingly comfortable and classy, along with being totally tough and practical.

Ford's base half-ton pickup in 1984 and continued on as the main force to be reckoned with in the pickup market.

The F-series pickup became the world's best-selling nameplate of all time in 1995 after roaring past the VW Beetle. More than 26 million F-series trucks had been sold by 1997, some worked to death by their owners, and others treated to a more civilized existence. "Today's F-series competes in a marketplace that has changed considerably since the nameplate's introduction in 1948," said Ford strategic market analysis manager Joel Pitcoff. "No longer strictly a workhorse, the present [F-150] has taken its place as a family member and a pleasure companion." And it looked so darn good, too.

Yet another new and improved F-150 appeared for 2004 to help keep Ford's winning streak intact. How much longer it runs remains up to Chevrolet. Or, eventually, maybe even Toyota.

The Pickup Game

Chapter 1

Ford kicks things off in 1925

Henry Ford was the man behind so many transportation milestones, not the least of which was putting the masses on wheels. By building the affordable Model T by the millions, ol' Henry helped thoroughly transform both the newborn automotive industry and the American way of life, neither of which have slowed down since. But commonly overlooked are his various high-flying feats. He also was the first to privately offer regularly scheduled airmail delivery, the first to offer air-freight service, the first to build a paved airport runway, the first to hire flight attendants, the first to operate a cross-country airline network—all this from a mover and shaker who was deathly afraid of leaving the ground. Simply put, getting people from point A to B as easily and cheaply as possible was Ford's obsession, regardless of whether it was wheels, propellers, or whatever supplying the momentum.

Delivering goods from A to B was another Ford focus. Also among his long list of historic firsts is credit for kicking off the Big Three truck race, although this momentous occasion didn't come about until 1917, 14 years after the Ford Motor Company was born. Why the lag time?

It wasn't that he was blind to the opportunity of selling more gas-powered contraptions. Commercial vehicles, in fact, were among his earliest experiments. His first business venture, the Detroit Automobile Company founded in August 1899, rolled out its first product, an enclosed delivery wagon, in January 1900. But Detroit Automobile was dead within the year. Next, in November 1901, came the Henry Ford Company, which Henry left behind in March 1902. The Ford firm we know today was established in June 1903, and two years later the boss was again testing the utility field, this time with the "Model C fitted with our Delivery Top." Its price was a relatively steep $950, explaining why only 10 or so were built.

Ford didn't offer another commercial vehicle until 1912. This $700 delivery car featured a unique delivery body and was "tougher than an army of mules and cheaper than a team of horses." But it too failed to bring customers running and was quickly discontinued. Of more significant note that year was another new model, a "commercial roadster" featuring a removable rumble seat that allowed for additional hauling space in back. Creative customers then took it from there. Out went the rumble seat, in went a home-built cargo box, and presto, a Model T pickup.

Quick-thinking entrepreneurs also began offering similar load-conscious modifications. Most prominent perhaps was the Smith Form-a-Truck kit, which in 1913 turned a polite Model T into a lengthened, chain-driven, one-ton workhorse. Countless other aftermarket conversions soon followed, with various cheap, simple, slip-in cargo boxes being sold through many outlets. This mom-and-pop cottage industry flourished during the twentieth century's second decade before Henry Ford finally decided to stop standing by while outsiders collected revenues that he could be raking in.

Ford officially entered the truck business on July 27, 1917, announcing the availability of its new Model TT, a one-ton machine sold in bare-chassis form only. Though still a modified passenger-car platform, it nonetheless offered rugged qualities that only a truck could. Its reinforced frame rolled on a wheelbase measuring two feet longer than the Model T's. Suspension components in back were beefed up, and a truly tough worm-drive axle was installed, as were artillery-type rear wheels wearing solid rubber tires. All this additional might made the Model TT an overnight success. Ford sold 100,000 one-ton chassis by 1919.

Big bare-chassis trucks were the only choices from Ford into the Twenties. Adding cabs and beds continued to be left up to the aftermarket, reportedly because Henry didn't want to face a bad-press backlash should he start putting defenseless ma-and-pa outfits out of business. Creating a light-duty half-ton vehicle also remained an aftermarket staple.

Then the main man changed his mind. Or perhaps he noticed that arch-rivals Chevrolet and Dodge, too, were finding success in the truck market; the latter after introducing its "screenside" commercial car late in 1917, the former after rolling out both half- and one-ton bare-chassis vehicles the following year. To stay ahead of the competition, Ford in October 1923 announced it finally would begin offering factory-direct bodies for the TT chassis. And an even more important proclamation followed two years later when Ford introduced its "Model T Runabout with Pick-Up Body," the forerunner to all those sharp-looking, incredibly comfortable, fully functional utility vehicles now dominating the Detroit scene.

Creating Ford's first pickup in 1925 was just so darned easy. That cargo box simply bolted right in place of the roadster's rear deck. Beneath it went a heavier nine-leaf buggy spring to help hold up the load. Being such a cinch to install, the Pick-Up Body also was made available as an individual option, priced at $25, for any Model T roadster.

With both the Model TT one-ton and the light-duty Model T pickup, Ford quickly established itself as America's leading truck builder, controlling about 75 percent of the market by 1926. Model T half-ton production was 33,795 in 1925, followed by 75,406 in 1926 and 28,142 in 1927 before the Model T era finally came to a close.

Ford's truck legacy began in July 1917 when the company announced its Model TT one-ton chassis. Additional bodywork was left up to the aftermarket at first. A factory-direct pickup-style body was introduced in 1923, followed by an open C-cab in January 1924 and an eight-foot stake bed in December that year. A 1921 Model TT is shown here.

> ### 1917 Model TT
> **Wheelbase: 124 inches**
> **Weight: 1,450 pounds**
> **Price: $600 (sold as bare-chassis only)**
> **Engine: 176.7-cubic-inch L-head inline**
>   **four-cylinder**
> **Output: 20 horsepower**
> **Production: 209**

Ford's long-running L-head four-cylinder was rated at various levels during the Model T's equally long stay on the market from 1909 to 1927. The rating for this 1921 Model TT's engine was 20 horsepower.

Heavy-duty, speed-limiting, worm-drive rear axles were staples beneath big trucks, like Ford's one-ton Model TT, during the Teens and Twenties.

Chevrolet kicked off its truck legacy in January 1918 with two new offerings, the one-ton Model T and half-ton Model 490, both sold without cab or bed. The 1918 Model 490 pickup shown here features custom-built wooden bodywork.

Rival Responses:

1918 Chevrolet Model 490
Model: 1/2-ton truck, sold as chassis only
Wheelbase: 102 inches
Engine: 26-hp 171-cid four-cylinder
Price: $595
Weight: 2,170 pounds

1918 Dodge Brothers "Screenside"
Model: 1/2-ton commercial car
Wheelbase: 114 inches
Engine: 35-hp 212-cid four-cylinder
Price: $885
Weight: 2,620 pounds

The company founded by John and Horace Dodge in 1914 began supplying the U.S. Army with trucks in 1916. The Dodge Brothers firm's first civilian truck, actually a half-ton commercial car, debuted in October 1917. It was called a "screenside" for obvious reasons. Dodge became a division of Chrysler Corporation in 1928.

On April 15, 1925, Ford announced the arrival of its "Model T Runabout with Pick-Up Body," America's first factory-delivered, steel-bodied pickup truck. Base price for this half-ton truck was $281. The wire wheels shown here actually became an option in 1926. Wood-spoke rims were the norm in 1925.

1925 Model T pickup
Wheelbase: 100 inches
Weight: 1,471 pounds
Price: $281
Engine: 176.7-cubic-inch L-head inline
    four-cylinder
Output: 20 horsepower
Production: 33,795

Supplied by Ruckstell, this two-speed axle option doubled the 1925 Model T pickup's gear choices.

The same engine powered both the big, burly Model TT and its more civilized Model T pickup cousin. Advertised output for the 176.7-cubic-inch four-cylinder in 1925 remained at 20 horsepower.

The Pick-Up Body was offered separately and as an individual option, priced at $25, in 1925. When purchased separately, the box was painted black. When installed at the factory, the color was the same as the cab.

Model T Roadster Pickup Numbers		
Year	Production	Base Price
1925	33,795	$281
1926	75,406	$361
1927	28,142	$381

What you saw was what you got inside a Model T roadster pickup. Not only was the interior spartan, to say the least, notice that you couldn't even enter from the driver's side thanks to the spare tire location. At least side curtains were available.

Model T upgrades for 1926
Chassis height lowered 1.5 inches
One-piece windshield for coupe and Tudor models
Longer hood with more louvers
Nickel-plated headlight rims
More integrated cowl
Wider, longer fenders
Wider running boards
Fuel tank moved beneath cowl (from beneath driver's seat) on all models except Fordor

Ford announced as many as 81 updates for the 1926 Model T. New fenders and wider running boards were added, and overall impressions were cleaned up by reshaping the cowl to better follow the hood line. A cowl vent was also new, as were additional louvers in the hood panels.

The Model T pickup price went up to $366 in 1926, $381 with optional balloon tires. Chassis refinements included raised spindles and revised springs, which all helped lower the Model T by 1.5 inches. The pedal-operated, self-energizing service brake in the transmission was enlarged.

Look Ma, no brakes. Model T Fords featured only rear-wheel brakes. Mechanical stoppers at all four wheels didn't appear until the new Model A was introduced in December 1927.

A heavier nine-leaf buggy spring helped hold up the Model T pickup's tail. Larger brakes were added in 1926 (shown here) as the lever-operated rear drums' diameters went from eight inches to eleven.

Model T Fords were converted into various kinds of utility vehicles during the Twenties, including "hucksters," the forerunners of the modern station wagon. Wooden huckster bodies were offered by aftermarket companies or were hand-built by the vehicle's owner, as was the case for this 1926 model.

1926 Model T engine
Type: inline L-head four-cylinder
Bore & stroke: 3.75 x 4 inches
Displacement: 176.7 cubic inches
Compression: 4.0:1
Horsepower: 22 at 1,600 rpm
Carburetor: Kingston or Holley one-barrel

Depot hacks hauled luggage at rail stations. It was the huckster's job to take the goods from the farm to the market.

An optional heater in the 1926 Model T's case meant a quilt that, like the wooden huckster bodywork surrounding it, was handmade.

Model T headlights in 1925 were mounted on the frame rail horns. New fenders appeared in 1926, and the headlights were then mounted on them. For 1927, a stylish front fender tie-bar was incorporated, and this bar also served as a mounting point for the headlights. Notice the leather strap used to keep the starter crank in place.

1927 Model T pickup colors
- **Commercial Green (with black fenders)**
- **Black (body and fenders)**
NOTE: Other colors were available for Model T automobiles in 1927

Model T pickup power in 1927 still came from Ford's 176.7-cubic-inch L-head four-cylinder, now producing 22 maximum horsepower at 1,600 rpm. Compression was 3.98:1. Notice the nickel-plated radiator shell—like those headlight rims, it was introduced in 1926 as an option on open models.

In typical Model T fashion, Ford's 1927 pickup was controlled by three foot pedals, each identified by a letter signifying its purpose. On the left (C) is the high/low clutch, in the middle (R) is the reverse actuator, on the right (B) is the brake.

More optional color choices appeared for the Model T in 1927, and the optional wire wheels from 1926 were made a standard feature. Joining the standard Commercial Green paint (shown here) were black, blue, and brown.

Model T Milestones
October 8, 1908: Model T introduced as 1909 model
1911: four-cylinder engine revised with covers for valve stems and springs
1919: electric starter introduced as option
May 25, 1927: Model T assembly ends after 15,007,033 built

The cargo box for the Model T pickup was 56 inches long, 13 inches deep, and 40.75 inches wide. In typical pickup fashion, the box also featured four stake holes and a drop-down tailgate.

This was it as far as dashboard instruments and controls went in 1927. The electric self-starter was a new standard feature in 1927. Next to it is the ammeter.

Battling the Bow-Tie

Chapter 2

Trading the sales lead through the Thirties

The great American pickup wasted little time hauling butt into the future after Ford historically defined the breed (from a modern perspective) in 1925. Within five years, both Dodge—by then a division of Chrysler Corporation—and Chevrolet had followed suit with factory-complete, steel-bodied half-tons of their own. They then were joined during the Thirties by comparable commercial vehicles from the likes of International-Harvester, Studebaker, Reo, and even Mack, resulting in a light-truck field that was every bit as crowded as the one we know today.

The Big Three, however, still stole the show 60-some years back. More than half of the 600,000 trucks built in this country in 1937 wore Chevrolet, Ford, or Dodge badges. The majority of these were pickups, and most by far were from Chevy and Ford, leading more than one casual witness nowadays to point out that "Big Three" was in truth a misnomer during the light-truck race's earliest decades. In those days Dodge wasn't just third, it was a distant, distant third.

The gap between first and second also was rather wide during the early Twenties. Total Chevrolet truck production to date surpassed 100,000 in June 1925, a notable achievement, sure. But Ford had sold that many Model TT one-tons alone by 1919, and the entrenched industry leader picked up the annual pace further after the half-ton Model T roadster made history six years later. In 1925 Dearborn rolled out more than 33,000 soft-top pickups, a total that on its own surpassed Chevy's entire truck run (all sizes, all styles) for the year.

The challenger then caught the long-time champ in 1927 and held the top spot another year before Ford rose back up, with its new Model A, to reclaim its rightful throne. The two titans traded blows from there as Chevy grabbed the lead again in 1933, 1934, and 1936, Ford in 1935 and 1937.

Once in its soon-to-be-customary place atop the goods-hauling heap, Chevrolet then proceeded to win sales battle after sales battle through one worldwide war, one police action in Korea, and into one escalating military intervention in Southeast Asia. A dozen New York Yankee world championships, five presidents, and one baby boom later, Ford managed to bring an end to Chevy's winning streak. And today it's the Blue-Oval band doing all the horn blowing concerning its unbeatable status.

While the Model A's appearance in 1928 made major headlines, easily the biggest breakthrough in Ford pickup ranks prior to World War II came in 1932 when ol' Henry introduced his "eight for the price of four." Chevrolet had wowed the low-priced ranks with its "Cast Iron Wonder," an overhead-valve straight-six, in 1929. Ford then did Chevy two better with its "flathead" V8 milestone. While the company's steady four-cylinder remained in production, the 221-cubic-inch L-head eight provided an affordable alternative to truck-buyers in the need for more speed. Costing only about $100 more than the four, the first flathead V8 produced 65 horsepower, compared to 50 for its little L-head cousin.

Various upgrades had the Ford V8 producing 85 horsepower by 1934. Then along came a second, smaller flathead in 1937, undoubtedly in response to ever-present requests for a Ford six, queries that grew more prominent each year after Dearborn dropped its long-trusted four-cylinder early in 1934. Offering "four-cylinder economy combined with eight-cylinder smoothness," this 136-cid V8 was brought over from the European market

where it had been motivating Brits and Frenchmen for a year.

Maximum output was predictably less at 60 horsepower, while fuel economy was equally predictable: roughly 25 mpg, up from the 20 to 22 cruising mpg normally encountered by drivers of the larger flathead. Saving at the gas pump was the main attraction, but interest quickly waned once drivers found that the so-called V8/60 could hardly get out of its own way. The little V8/60 was history by 1941, the year Ford finally introduced a six.

In other pre-war truck news, a closed-cab pickup body joined the existing roadster model in August 1928 as the Model A replaced the Model T. The quaint open-air pickup then faded into the sunset, last appearing in 1934. Car-line styling touches also began to disappear, though Ford pickups continued carrying leftover automobile sheetmetal up through 1936. A distinctive truck-only look debuted in 1937, announced prominently up front with an unforgettable "barrel" grille. These barrel-nose models rolled on into 1939, then were superseded by pickups that once again looked like their car counterparts—but that wasn't a bad thing at all considering how many critics still love the 1940 Ford facade.

Another restyling segregated the pickup from the passenger car again in 1942 before World War II temporarily interrupted production of both lines. Ford trucks then had to wait four years before resuming the chase.

Like its Model T forerunner, the Model A pickup was offered in roadster form. But new for the A-based truck in 1928 was an available closed cab. The roadster shown here was one of 35,825 open-cab Ford pickups built for 1929.

Thirties Truck Race (based on annual new registrations)		
	Ford	Chevrolet
1930	197,100	118,300
1931	138,854	99,600
1932	66,937	60,784
1933	62,397	99,880
1934	128,250	157,507
1935	185,848	167,129
1936	177,244	204,344
1937	189,376	183,674
1938	100,959	119,479
1939	128,889	169,457
NOTE: numbers included all models, all sizes		

(Above) Also based on its car models, Chevrolet's earliest pickup line featured a roadster model. Shown here is a 1930 model. Chevy's last roadster pickup was sold in 1932.

(Right) Chevrolet first grabbed the truck sales lead in 1927 as Ford production slowed in preparation for the new Model A's 1928 introduction. Then Chevy countered Ford's move with its new six-cylinder engine in 1929. Displacement was 194 cubic inches.

This closed-cab Chevrolet pickup initially sold for $470 in 1932. That price then dropped to $440 later in the year.

Rival Responses: Chevrolet Truck Milestones

1929: overhead-valve inline six-cylinder engine introduced

November 1930: Martin-Parry body company purchased by GM; factory-complete, fully enclosed Chevy pickups became available soon afterward

1932: last roadster pickup offered

1933: 1 millionth truck sold

1934: truck-only styling first applied

1936: wood construction last used in truck cabs midyear

1937: OHV six-cylinder treated to major redesign

Like Chevrolet's second-series pickups of 1936, its 1937 models (shown here) featured modern hydraulic brakes at all four corners.

Sealed-beam headlights became standard equipment for the attractive 1940 Chevrolet pickup.

Simplicity was the order of the day inside a 1929 Ford pickup. Consider that the fuel gauge basically was a window that looked directly into the cowl-mounted fuel tank.

(Left) Unlike the typical folding top on a 1929 Model A car, the roof on Ford's roadster pickup lifted off "as is."

1928 Model A
Wheelbase: 103.5 inches
Weight: 2,063 pounds (roadster), 2,073 pounds (closed cab), 1,633 pounds (bare chassis)
Price: $395 (roadster), $445 (closed cab), $325 (bare chassis)
Engine: 200.5-cubic-inch L-head inline four-cylinder
Output: 40 horsepower
Production: 23,972 (roadster), 47,212 (closed cab), 42,612 (bare chassis)

1930 Ford Truck Colors
Black
Blue Rock Green
Rock Moss Green
Menelas Orange
Pegex Orange
Phoenix Brown
Rubellite Red

The most popular Ford pickup in 1930 was the closed-cab version, priced at $455. Production was 86,383.

Early 1930 Ford pickups were simply 1929 leftovers. A restyled Model A truck body then appeared midyear, followed by the same cargo box seen the year before.

Car-line styling touches continued carrying over into light-truck ranks in 1930.

Bare bones was again a fair description for a Ford pickup interior in 1930. Notice the flip-out windshield.

Powering a Ford pickup in 1930 was this 200.5-cubic-inch L-head four-cylinder, rated at 40 horsepower. Compression was 4.22:1.

(Below) The Model AA 1.5-ton replaced its one-ton Model TT predecessor in 1928. Shown here is a 1931 Model AA.

The Model A pickup in 1930 closely resembled its automotive cousin, appearing in cabriolet form at right. Although the two lines still shared much sheetmetal, Ford's cars and trucks began looking notably different soon afterward. A distinctive sloping grille set the 1935 pickup (left) apart from its rather mundane 1934 predecessor.

1930 Ford Model A Utility Vehicle Production	
Chassis	58,708
Town Car delivery	3
Sedan delivery	7,132
Roadster pickup	3,429
Closed-cab pickup	86,383
Panel delivery	14,063
Drop-floor panel	17
Special delivery	19
Station wagon	3,510

Ford finally closed the door on its roadster pickup in 1934. Only 347 topless trucks were built that year.

1934 Model 46
Wheelbase: 112 inches
Weight: 2,386 pounds
Price: $445 (closed cab)
Engine: 200.5-cubic-inch L-head inline four-cylinder (discontinued in March 1934); 221-cubic-inch L-head V8
Output: 50 horsepower (four-cylinder); 85 horsepower (V8)

Ford dropped its four-cylinder engine in March 1934, leaving only the 85-horsepower flathead V8 to power its pickup trucks.

Ford introduced America's first low-priced eight in 1932 for both car and truck lines. Nicknamed "flathead" for rather obvious reasons, this V8 (at right) displaced 221 cubic inches. Initial output was pegged at 65 horse-power. A smaller 136-cubic-inch flathead V8 (left) appeared in 1937, rated at 60 horsepower.

The 1934 Ford's cargo box was 69.75 inches long, 44 inches wide.

Roadster Pickup Production	
1928 Model A	23,972
1929 Model A	35,825
1930 Model A	3,429
1931 Model A	2,637
1932 Model B	593
1933 Series 46	n/a
1934 Series 46	347

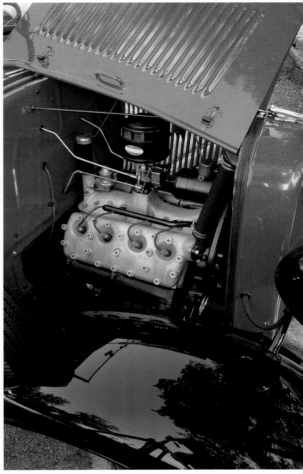

Interiors were still Plain Jane in 1934.

V8 output increased from 75 horsepower to 85 in 1934. Additional improvements that year included a cast-alloy crankshaft and a new dual-throat carburetor, the Stromberg 48, on a redesigned dual-plane intake manifold. Compression for this 221-cubic-inch V8 was 6.33:1.

A gracefully sloping radiator announced a new Ford pickup's presence in 1935.

1935 Model 48
Wheelbase: 112 inches
Price: $480
Engine: 221-cubic-inch L-head V8
Output: 85 horsepower

Ford's "V8/85" remained the only power source for Ford trucks in 1935.

This is what aftermarket "air conditioning" looked like in 1935.

Ford's pickup cab became an all-steel unit in 1935 as the wood floor used previously was finally deleted. The pickup's price that year was $480.

Car-like styling reappeared for Ford pickups in 1940 after temporarily falling by the wayside in 1937. The grilles interchanged between Ford cars and trucks in 1940, front fenders didn't—pickup versions featured straightened trailing edges, required to mate up with the more angular truck cab.

<u>1940 Model 01C (V8/85) and 02C (V8/60)</u>

Wheelbase: 112 inches (half-ton), 122 inches (3/4-ton)

Weight: 2,373 pounds (01C), 2,542 pounds (02C),

Price: $595 (01C), $610 (02C)

Engine: 221-cubic-inch L-head V8 (01C), 136-cubic-inch L-head V8 (02C)

Output: 85 horsepower (01C), 60 horsepower (02C)

The steering column shifter seen here is a non-stock, owner-installed feature borrowed from Ford's 1940 passenger-car line. Correct for the 1940 pickup's three-speed manual was a floor-shifter. A floor-shifted four-speed was also optional that year.

All Ford pickups from 1934 to 1940 were V8-powered. An optional six-cylinder, the company's first since 1908, appeared in 1941. The small 136-cubic-inch V8/60 was discontinued after 1940. Shown here is that year's V8/85.

An extra taillight and a chromed rear bumper were optional features in 1940. This model also features an optional Columbia overdrive rear axle.

<u>1940 Truck Options</u>
Chrome rear bumper
Side-mount spare tire
Wheel trim rings
Radio
White sidewall tires
Grille guard
Spotlight
Passenger-side windshield wiper
Passenger-side sun visor
Fender skirts

Headlight bezels on Ford pickups in 1940 were painted. They were commonly chromed on passenger cars that year.

Wide whitewalls weren't typical on any pickup in 1940, but adding them certainly was a possibility. The bright trim rings seen here were optional that year.

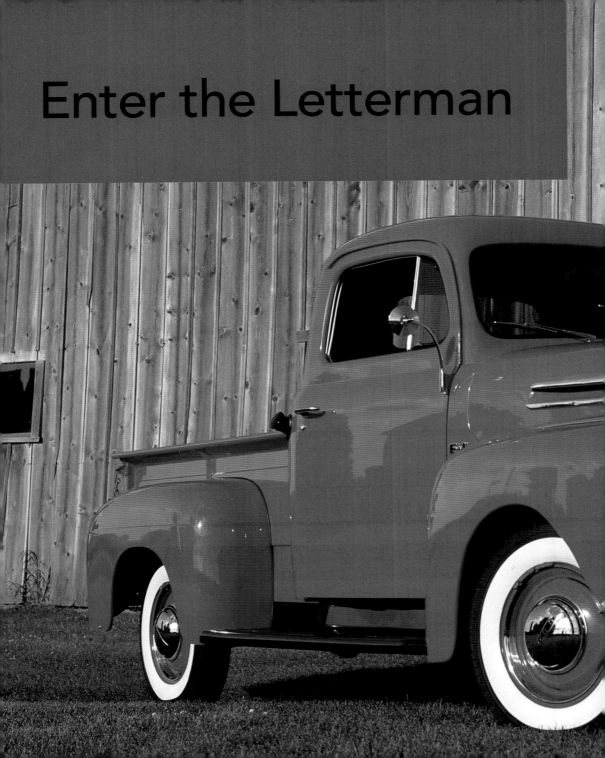

Enter the Letterman

Chapter 3

Ford's F-1, 1948–1952

Now the firmly established industry leader, Chevrolet beat its Big Three rivals out of the blocks with America's first all-new postwar pickup in 1947. These Advance Design models continued to be this country's best-selling trucks right up until their retirement early in 1955, even though few notable changes were made during their time on the market. Not even Ford's fabulously redesigned F-100, introduced for 1953, could unseat Chevrolet's pickups at the top of the sales heap.

Ford resumed peacetime production of light trucks in May 1945, rolling out basically the same restyled model seen all too briefly in 1942 before World War II curtailed civilian vehicle manufacturing. Upgrades were minor, including improved steering, wider frame rails, and grease fittings for the universal joints. This package then rolled on with few additional changes up through 1947. Better brakes appeared in 1946, and that was about it as far as progress was concerned.

Ford's response to the Advance Design Chevy appeared in January 1948 wearing badges as new as the trucks themselves. Dearborn's first F-series truck line started off with the F-1 1/2-ton. Labels read F-2 for 3/4-ton models, F-3 for 1-tons, and so on. The numbering ran all the way up to F-8 for the biggest rigs.

Freshened styling was only the beginning as far as the 1948 F-1 was concerned. Ford people didn't call these pickups "Bonus Built" trucks for nothing. Getting more machine for your money was the idea, and to that end Dearborn reportedly invested $1 million to improve ergonomics, a term not yet invented then but clearly applicable from a modern perspective. The appropriately named "Million Dollar Cab" featured what promotional folks called "Living-Room" comfort. This cab was not only taller, it also was widened by seven inches to make room for a third rider. All three could enter and exit with little worry of knocking knees on the door hinges thanks to doors relocated three inches farther forward.

A taller, one-piece, flat windshield and enlarged rear glass aided visibility. And new seats with better springs and improved adjustment ranges enticed potential customers inside the F-1's cab with what Ford admen liked to call "Easy Chair Comfort." Also enhancing comfort inside was the new Level Action Cab suspension system, which used rubber cab mounts to help insulate passengers from shocks sent through the frame. All told, the F-1 was definitely a better-riding, easier-to-drive truck.

Mechanicals carried over from 1947, but that didn't stop Ford's biggest, roomiest pickup yet from selling like relative hotcakes. Sales-wise, this was the best year for Ford truck sales since 1929. The total 1948 count for all models, light to heavy, was 301,791. F-1 pickup production was 108,806.

Ford's original F-series held down the fort until the redesigned F-100 appeared for 1953. F-1 pickups received a fresh face in 1951, featuring a new toothy grille that rolled over into 1952. Various minor engineering changes were made in 1951, but the biggest mechanical news came the following year when the antiquated L-head six-cylinder was finally replaced by a modern overhead-valve six. This 215-cubic-inch engine produced 101 horsepower. The flathead V8, meanwhile, soldiered on, just as it would again in 1953. V8 output for 1952 was boosted to 106 horsepower thanks to a new cam with more lift.

Chevrolet was the first of the Big Three truck builders to offer a truly new postwar pickup, introducing its Advance Design models in the summer of 1947. This 1953 Chevrolet half-ton is equipped with the optional five-window cab, which featured two extra windows at each rear corner.

Ford's light trucks were restyled for 1942 before World War II shut down civilian vehicle production early that year. This body, with its "waterfall" grille, then reappeared in May 1945 when peacetime manufacturing resumed and continued on basically unchanged up through 1947.

1946 Pickup

Wheelbase: 114 inches

Width: 72.14 inches

Height: 71.45 inches

Shipping weight: 2,966 pounds

Gross vehicle weight: 4,700 pounds

Base price: $961 (w/six-cylinder); $1,022 (w/V8)

Engine: 90-horsepower, 226-cubic-inch L-head inline six-cylinder, standard; 100-horsepower 239-cubic-inch L-head V8, optional

Transmission: three-speed manual; four-speed manual and overdrive, optional

Tires: 6.50 x 16

Production: 75,088

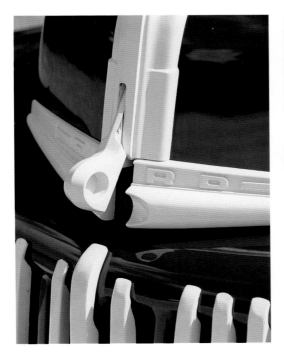 

An easily handled hood latch was cleverly incorporated into the trim work on the nose of 1942–'47 Ford pickups. In 1942, the FORD lettering was contrasted in black; this area was monochromatic (in crème) on following models.

Both a six-cylinder and this flathead V8 were offered for Ford pickups in 1946. The L-head six displaced 226 cubic inches and produced 90 horsepower. The 239-cubic-inch V8 was rated at 100 horsepower.

Production of 1946 Ford pickups (shown here) was 75,088. Passenger-car-style hubcaps were standard this year.

The F-series line featured Ford's first completely redesigned cab since 1938. F-1 production in 1949 (shown here) was 104,803. The red pinstripe seen on the F-1's grille in 1948 did not return the following year.

1948 F-1

Wheelbase: 114 inches
Length: 188.8 inches
Width: 75.94 inches
Height: 75.64 inches
Shipping weight: 3,061 pounds
Gross vehicle weight: 4,700 pounds
Base price: $1,239
Engine: 90-horsepower, 226-cubic-inch L-head inline six-cylinder, standard; 100-horsepower 239-cubic-inch L-head V8, optional
Transmission: three-speed manual; heavy-duty three- and four-speed manuals, optional
Tires: 6.50 x 16
Rear axle ratio: 3.78:1 (4.27:1, optional)
Production: 108,006

Chevrolet beat its Big Three rivals out of the blocks with an all-new postwar pickup in 1947. Ford's response then appeared the following year wearing all-new F-series labels that varied by load capacity. The 1/2-ton was an "F-1," the 3/4-ton was an "F-2," and so on.

F-1 wheels were painted black in 1948. In 1949 they were colored to match each individual truck's exterior paint choice.

1950 F-1 Paint Choices
Silvertone Gray
Sheridan Blue
Meadow Green
Palisade Green
Vermilion
Black

Telling a 1950 F-1 apart from its 1949 forerunner was not easy at a glance, since no major changes were made on the outside. F-1 pickup production in 1950 was 148,956.

(Above) A chrome rear bumper was an F-1 option in 1950. The F-1 base price that year was $1,256.

(Left) One of the quickest ways to identify a 1950 F-1 requires a look inside, where the standard three-speed manual transmission's shifter was relocated from the floor to the steering column.

The F-series truck's nose was restyled for 1951. The F-1 pickup's base price that year was $1,286. Both chromed and argent-painted headlight rims appeared in 1951. Cream-coloring also replaced the grille's argent finish late in the year. The chrome hubcaps seen in 1951 were replaced the following year by argent-painted pieces to meet material restrictions imposed by Washington due to the Korean War.

<u>**1951 F-1 Paint Choices**</u>
Black
Sheridan Blue
Alpine Blue
Sea Island Green
Silvertone Gray
Meadow Green
Vermilion

Beauty beneath the F-series truck's mildly refashioned skin in 1951 included improved steering and suspension components and various upgraded engine parts. The L-head six received thickened main bearings, a revised camshaft, an aluminum timing gear, and a new intake manifold. The six-cylinder's water pump, too, was updated.

The 100-horsepower, 239-cubic-inch flathead V8 remained an option in 1951 but was refitted with various fresh parts like the standard six-cylinder. The V8's water pump, cam, valve rotators, and offset piston pins were all new.

A revised dash layout appeared in 1951 as part of the F-series truck's new Five Star Cab. Optional was a plusher Five Star Extra Cab, featuring lots of extra insulation and sound deadener and various upscale appointments.

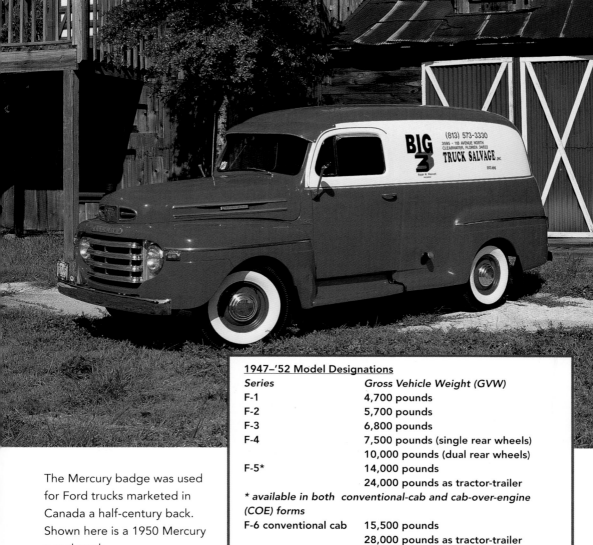

The Mercury badge was used for Ford trucks marketed in Canada a half-century back. Shown here is a 1950 Mercury panel truck.

1947–'52 Model Designations

Series	Gross Vehicle Weight (GVW)
F-1	4,700 pounds
F-2	5,700 pounds
F-3	6,800 pounds
F-4	7,500 pounds (single rear wheels)
	10,000 pounds (dual rear wheels)
F-5*	14,000 pounds
	24,000 pounds as tractor-trailer

available in both conventional-cab and cab-over-engine (COE) forms

F-6 conventional cab	15,500 pounds
	28,000 pounds as tractor-trailer
F-6 COE	16,000 pounds
	28,000 as tractor-trailer
F-7	19,000 pounds
	35,000 pounds as tractor-trailer
F-8	21,500 pounds
	39,000 pounds as tractor-trailer

Canadian-marketed Mercury trucks traded the "F" designation for "M."

Ford's first F-series model line began with the F-1 half-ton and topped out with the three-ton F-8 big-rig. A 1951 F-8 hauls the goods to market here.

Making History

Chapter 4

The fabulous F-100 debuts in 1953

As impressive as Ford's thoroughly modern F-series pickups were, they still couldn't quite turn heads away from America's best-selling trucks, still built by Chevrolet. The F-1, in fact, actually lost ground as Chevy's Advance Design models gained even more steam going into the Fifties. Ford's second-place market share came in like clockwork at about 21 percent from 1946 to 1949, before jumping up to more than 27 in 1950. Chevrolet's prime cut, meanwhile, was notably on the rise every year: 26.8 percent in 1947, 29.2 in 1948, and a whopping 35.2 in 1949. In 1950 the percentage point gap between the top two slots in this country's truck sales rankings almost reached 9 points. It hit 10 points the following year, and surpassed 11 in 1952. Chevy clearly was getting away. But fortunately Ford designers had more than your basic makeover in mind for 1953.

This time around, Dearborn reportedly shelled out $30 million for what arguably represented Detroit's earliest application of an ergonomic study in a pickup truck design project. If not the earliest, it certainly was the most comprehensive up to that point. For 1953, designers were asked to create the safest, most comfortable, easiest-to-drive, hardest working half-ton ever. Stylists also were heavily involved, with the goal being to balance form and function like no other pickup before. The result was the renamed F-100, a milestone pickup if there ever was one.

The bulk of those bucks were spent on the F-100's "Driver Engineered" cab, which was developed using the "Measuring Man," a life-size model of Average Joe Trucker. Improved instrument and control locations, sound deadener in the doors, an even wider seat than the F-1's with better shock-absorbing characteristics—new "Driverized" features like these guaranteed Average Joe, as well as his passengers, would feel right at home. Incorporated, too, was an enlarged, one-piece, curved windshield, which worked in concert with a new four-foot-wide rear window to equal a 55 percent increase in total glass area. Extra glass meant added safety through better visibility, and it also translated into added style.

According to advertisements, the 1953 F-100 offered truck buyers "more power, more comfort, more economy." In the humble opinion of legendary *Mechanix Illustrated* road tester Tom McCahill, the new and improved seat was "as comfortable as the average sedan's." Operational impressions were also sedan-like, thanks to various steering gear improvements. Most noticeable was a steering wheel relocated at a better angle to reduce driver fatigue. Engineers also moved the front axle backward to better balance the vehicle, and this change in turn reduced the truck's turning radius by about 19 percent.

Additional momentous mechanical upgrades included, as brochures announced, "The Greatest Transmission Choice in Truck History." Five gearboxes were offered, beginning with a standard synchromesh three-speed. A heavy-duty three-speed, a three-speed with overdrive, a four-speed with "grannie" low, and the Fordomatic automatic were optional. The latter was a first for Ford's truck line and was listed only for half-ton F-series pickups in 1953.

F-100 power sources carried over essentially unchanged from 1952, with only revised motor mounts and larger radiators joining the carry-over 215-cubic-inch Cost Clipper six and 239-cubic-inch flathead V8 in 1953. Both of these were superseded the following year as an enlarged, higher-compression OHV six appeared, displacing 223 cubic inches. Output was 110 horsepower. The big news, though, involved the appearance of Ford's totally new OHV V8, which like Henry's tired old "flattie," also displaced 239 cubic inches. Output for this so-called Y-block V8 was 130 horsepower.

Although truly new inside and out, the F-100 still couldn't overtake its entrenched rival, but it did make up much lost ground. Ford truck sales in 1953 broke a company record set in 1929, and market penetration that year soared to 28.6 percent, less than 7 points short of the long-time leader. Chevrolet's advantage fell to just 3 points in 1954, the year Ford established yet another all-time sales high on the way to achieving a 30-percent market share for the first time since World War II. The challenger then narrowly missed upsetting the champion in 1957 and 1959. During that latter year Ford introduced its first factory-direct four-wheel-drive pickup.

Other notable F-100 updates up to that point included a modern 12-volt electrical system and a trendy wraparound windshield in 1956. A new marketing manager, Lee Iacocca, arrived to oversee Ford truck sales in 1957, and the products he pushed that year were markedly restyled. Gone were all those compound curves, replaced by crisp lines and soft corners. Gone, too, were running boards and "pontoon" fenders, with the former items now hidden inside the doors. Rear pontoons carried over for the traditional "Flareside" model but disappeared like their counterparts up front on the trendsetting "Styleside."

Like Chevrolet's classic Cameo Carrier, built from 1955 to 1958, Ford's fully fresh Styleside pickup featured a cab-wide bed in back that now allowed designers to let body lines run uninterrupted from nose to tail. Although wags were quick to compare the 1957 F-100 to a rolling refrigerator, this breakthrough look still signaled the arrival of a new era in pickup fashion. Conventional "stepside" trucks did remain the popular choice for years to come. But Ford's flashier Styleside—along with its "slab-sided" knock-offs from Chevy and Dodge—quickly gained momentum as pickup buyers became more stylish during the Sixties.

Ford's next F-100 restyle was unveiled in 1961.

1953 F-100

Wheelbase: 110 inches

Length: 189.12 inches

Height: 75.3 inches

Weight: 3,102 pounds

Price: $1,330 (w/base six-cylinder)

Standard engine: 101-horsepower, 215-cubic-inch OHV six-cylinder

Optional engine: 110-horsepower, 239-cubic-inch L-head V8

Standard transmission: Synchro-Silent three-speed manual w/column shift

Optional transmissions: Synchro-Silent heavy-duty three-speed manual w/column shift, Synchro-Silent heavy-duty three-speed w/column shift, Synchro-Silent four-speed w/floor shifter, Fordomatic automatic

Production: 116,437

The 1953 F-100's lightly curved windshield offered drivers more than 400 square inches of additional viewing pleasure compared to the 1952 F-1's flat front glass. Dual wipers were standard, as were sealed-beam headlights with a foot-controlled dimmer switch.

New numbering for 1953 meant the F-100 now equated to Ford's 1/2-ton truck. The F-250 3/4-ton pickup replaced both the F-2 and F-3 lines seen in 1952. That year's F-4 became the F-350 in 1953.

Both Ford's car and truck lines commemorated the company's 50th anniversary with appropriately adorned horn rings in 1953. Henry Ford founded the company named after him in June 1903.

Cargo box capacity, at 45 cubic feet, carried over from the F-1 models into the F-100 era. A rear bumper was optional in 1953.

"All-New Ford Driverized Cabs...
...usher in a completely new era of truck riding comfort. They ride so easily, you handle the controls so easily, you won't believe you're riding in a truck. Every inch of these new Ford cabs has been designed to free the driver of truck fatigue, to make the driver's job easier, safer and more efficient. Less effort required for driving means drivers stay fresh longer, like their jobs better, do more and better work."

—1953 Ford truck brochure

While the foot pedals still protruded from the floor, the accelerator linkage was rerouted through the firewall for the F-100. Additional modifications included concealed goose-neck hinges that allowed the doors to open wider. Door seals and locks also were improved for added durability and strength.

A V8 model's presence was proudly announced in the F-100's grille. An inverted three-pointed star indicated the installation of the standard Cost Clipper six-cylinder, a carry-over from 1952. The six displaced 215 cubic inches and produced 101 horsepower.

While wheelbase went down (from 114 inches to 110) for the F-150, overall length increased slightly (from 188.78 inches to 189.12), compared to the last F-1. Cab height for the F-100 was 75.3 inches.

New 1953 Model Designations

Series	Gross Vehicle Weight (GVW)
F-100	4,800 pounds
F-250	6,900 pounds
F-350	7,100 and 9,500 pounds
F-500	14,000 pounds
F-600	16,000 pounds
F-700 "Big Job"	19,500 pounds
F-750 "Big Job"	19,500 pounds
F-800 "Big Job"	22,000 pounds
F-900 "Big Job"	27,000 pounds

Introduced in 1932, Ford's venerable flathead V8 made one final appearance in 1953. Displacement that year was 239 cubic inches. Advertised output was 110 horsepower.

Small hubcaps were standard in 1953, as were 15-inch wheels. Sixteen-inch rims were optional. Wheels were painted to match the exterior color choice.

Chevrolet didn't waste any time upstaging the 1953 F-100
(at right), introducing its totally new Task Force trucks in March
1955. Chevy's 1955 3100-series pickup (left) clearly borrowed
more than one styling cue from the division's equally new
passenger car.

1953 F-100 Paint Choices
Raven Black
Sheridan Blue
Glacier Blue
Light Green
Vermilion
Meadow Green
Dovetone Gray

New for 1953 was an optional automatic transmission, the Fordomatic, offered only for half-ton F-series trucks that year. This transmission had debuted for Ford passenger cars two years earlier.

Improved comfort was just one of many selling points concerning the 1953 F-100 that Ford advertised. Added convenience and driver friendliness, too, were major attractions. *1953 Ford brochure*

As in previous years, the basic F-100 in 1956 rolled on a 110-inch wheelbase and featured a 6.5-foot-long cargo box, as demonstrated here. New this year was an "Express" F-100 that rode on the F-250's 118-inch chassis and used a longer 8-foot bed.

Available 1956 F-100 Powertrains
133-horsepower, 223-cid inline six-cylinder, standard
167-horsepower, 272-cid overhead-valve V8, optional
Three-speed manual transmission, standard
Three-speed manual w/overdrive, optional
Three-speed medium-duty manual, optional
Four-speed manual, optional
Fordomatic automatic, optional

Hood badges changed each year for the F-100: the 1956 rendition appears here. Base price for the 1956 F-100 (with six-cylinder) was $1,521.

Ford's first automatic transmission appeared on the car side of the fence in 1951. The Fordomatic automatic then became a half-ton truck option in 1953. The bright grille was added in 1956 as part of the Custom Cab package.

1956 F-100 Paint Choices
Raven Black
Diamond Blue
Nocturne Blue
Colonial White (used w/two-tone option)
Meadowmist Green
Platinum Gray
Primer Gray
Vermilion
Meadow Green
Goldenrod Yellow
NOTE: a special-order paint option also was available

A wraparound windshield was added as part of Ford's "Leadership Look" restyle in 1956. Complementing this expansive glass was a new roof overhang that served as a sun visor.

Introduced in 1954, Ford's Y-block V8 initially displaced 239 cubic inches, same as the old flathead it replaced. New for the 1956 F-100 was an enlarged Y-block that displaced 272 cubes. Output was 176 horsepower.

Custom Cab appointments for the 1956 F100 included black and white upholstery with bolsters and facing color keyed to match exterior paint. Additional Custom Cab features included a special insulated header panel, extra sound deadener in the floor and rear cab wall sections, twin sun visors, a passenger-side armrest, a large dome light, and an illuminated cigar lighter. Bright trim also was added on the outside.

A dramatic makeover in 1957 did away with the F-100's pontoon fenders up front. And a new body did the same in back. Joining the typical stepside cargo box (now known as the Flareside) was the Styleside box with its cab-wide walls. Chevrolet's Cameo was the first to try this look (using fiberglass) in 1955. But Ford was the first to apply it in the mainstream using steel panels. Chevy's Fleetside trucks then copied the Styleside image in 1958.

By 1960, Styleside models were outselling their Flareside counterparts by more than a 4–1 margin. Base price (with six-cylinder) for the latter was $1,956. The former's bottom line began at $1,972.

<u>1957 F-100</u>

Wheelbase: 110 inches

Length (8-foot box): 189.1 inches

Height: 75.5 inches

Weight: 3,120 pounds (Flareside), 3,110 pounds (Styleside)

Price: $1,789 (both Flareside and Styleside, w/base six-cylinder)

Standard engine: 139-horsepower, 223-cubic-inch OHV six-cylinder

Optional engine: 171-horsepower, 272-cubic-inch L-head V8

Standard transmission: Synchro-Silent three-speed manual w/column shift

Optional transmissions: Synchro-Silent heavy-duty three-speed manual w/column shift, Synchro-Silent heavy-duty three-speed w/column shift, Synchro-Silent four-speed w/floor shifter, Fordomatic automatic

Production: 182,640

Yet another revised hood badge showed up for the F-100 in 1960. Two-wheel-drive F-100 production that year was 27,383 Flaresides, 113,875 Stylesides. Another 964 Flaresides and 4,334 Stylesides were built with four-wheel-drive.

(Below) New for the 1960 Custom Cab option was nylon-saran seat upholstery with a contrasting ribbed vinyl center section. Chrome rings also adorned the instruments.

Quad headlights replaced the F-100's dual units in 1958. A crossbar running between those headlights set the 1960 F-100 apart from its 1959 predecessor, as did a revised grille and twin air intakes recessed into the hood's leading edge.

<u>1959 F-100 4x4*</u>

also offered as 3/4-ton F-250

Wheelbase: 118 inches

Weight: 3,563 pounds, Flareside; 3,573 pounds, Styleside

Price: $2,537 (Flareside w/base six-cylinder), $2,553 (Styleside w/base six-cylinder)

Standard engine: 139-horsepower, 223 cubic-inch OHV six-cylinder

Optional engine: 186-horsepower, 292 cubic-inch L-head V8

Transmission: three-speed manual mated to two-speed transfer case; heavy-duty three-speed and four-speed manuals, optional

Front suspension: 45-inch-long seven-leaf springs, 950-pound capacity

Rear suspension: 52-inch-long seven-leaf springs, 1,025-pound capacity

Front axle: Spicer full-floating, 3000-pound capacity, 3.92:1 ratio

Rear axle: Ford, 3,300-pound capacity, 3.89:1 ratio

Tires: 6.70 x 15 inches

Custom Cab features in 1960 again included extra trim and special two-tone appointments inside. The Custom Cab option cost $77 that year.

Fifteen-inch four-ply white-sidewall tires were available as a $31 option in 1960. Small hubcaps were once again standard.

Ford entered the fledgling four-wheel-drive market in 1959, two years after General Motors did. Previous 4x4 Ford pickups were aftermarket conversions. *1959 Ford truck brochure*

While Styleside trucks featured taillights incorporated nicely within their rear bodywork, the more mundane Flareside models used simple bolt-on units typically mounted to each side of the tailgate. The side-mount spare tire was a $15 option in 1960.

Selected 1960 F-100 options	
Four-wheel drive	$567
Locking rear axle	$51
Rear bumper	$26
Custom Cab package	$77
Side-mount spare	$15
Power steering	$125
Wraparound rear window	$29
Tu-Tone paint	$27
Three-speed medium-duty manual trans	$81
Overdrive	$109
Four-speed manual transmission	$87
Fordomatic automatic transmission	$200

The F-100's V8 displaced 292 cubic inches in 1960. Output was 172 horsepower. The base 223-cubic-inch six that year produced 139 horsepower.

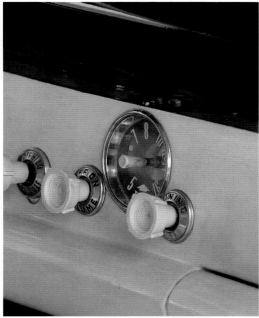

Various refinements came inside the 292-cubic-inch V8 in 1960, including revised combustion chambers and relocated spark plugs, both of which aided the engine's economical operation on regular-grade gasoline.

Like the MagicAire heater/defroster, turn signals, and windshield wipers, a transistor radio was optional for the F-100 in 1960.

Half 'n' Half

Chapter 5

Ranchero roundup, 1957–1979

The concept wasn't necessarily new when Ford combined car and truck to produce its first Ranchero. After all, the company's earliest pickups were all constructed similarly: an automobile in front, a cargo-carrying bed in back. But, prior to 1957, Detroit-watchers had never witnessed so much car-like comfort, convenience, and class teamed up with such pure practicality. No doubt about it, the Ranchero helped change the way Americans look at utility vehicles. Today's SUVs and crossovers both owe at least some portion of their existences to this milestone machine.

Ranchero roots ran back well before World War II and wrapped halfway around the world. In the early Thirties, Ford of Australia had begun marketing its "Utility" roadster—"Ute" for short. This was a Ford automobile with cargo-bed bodywork incorporated in back, a practical combination that would roll on in popular fashion Down Under up through 1958. It was the Ute that undoubtedly inspired designers back in Michigan to draw up a similar domestic model during the development stages for Ford's restyled 1952 line. Known as the "Roo Chaser" around Dearborn, this proposition was at first pooh-poohed then reconsidered a few years later when it came time for the 1957 remake. Helping seal the deal was the plain fact that the first Ranchero was so damned easy to build.

The Ford gang simply took a 1957 two-door Ranch Wagon and removed its rear roof section. The Ranchero and Ranch Wagon shared tailgates and rear compartment sub-floors. Unique to the former were the custom steel stampings for the cab roof, the upper cab rear panel, the double-walled cargo box, the bed floor, and the tailgate inner panel. Described by Ford as "America's first work or play truck," the 1957 Ranchero was marketed as a half-ton pickup. But, save for heavier springs, it was basically all Ford automobile beneath its certainly stylish skin—and that wasn't a bad thing.

"For the person who has always wanted a pickup, but is balked by the looks or ride qualities inherent in normal trucks, Ford has come to the rescue," announced a *Motor Life* review in 1957. As a pickup, the Ranchero could haul upwards of 1,190 pounds in its 32.4-cubic-foot cargo box. As a car, it could be dressed down with almost every optional bauble offered in 1957.

Production that first year hit 20,000, a figure that convinced Dearborn execs to keep this new breed around for more than a while. Ranchero remained in production up through 1979, and along the way it also inspired a copycat from Chevrolet, the El Camino. Born in 1959, Chevy's "car-truck" was briefly dropped after 1960 but then reappeared four years later and carried on quite successfully until early 1988.

Like its rival from Chevrolet, the Ranchero went through various transformations during its long career. In 1960 it was reintroduced as a compact Falcon, since affordability became the new key. "New way to vacation . . . Great way to save!" bragged ads that also claimed fuel economy of up to 30 mpg from the Falcon's 90-horse, 144-cubic-inch six-cylinder—the only available power source.

Ford's last Falcon-based Ranchero in 1966 served as a bridge of sorts between past and future. Whereas the 1960–'65 renditions had been officially labeled "Falcon Ranchero," this larger, flashier machine was known plain and simply as "Ranchero."

Dearborn decision-makers no longer wanted their half-breed to be associated with the budget-minded compact crowd. In 1967, it officially became a mid-sized Fairlane model.

Ranchero remained in Dearborn's intermediate ranks through evolutions as a Torino (until 1977), followed by an LTD II variant for its last three renditions. A full frame went back underneath in 1972 (unit-body construction was used from 1960 to 1971), and wheelbase was stretched back to 118 inches, where it had been before the 1960 downsizing.

Another redesign in 1977 transformed the last-generation Ranchero into easily the biggest of the breed. Still on a 118-inch wheelbase, this hefty machine measured 220.1 inches from nose to tail, 79.6 inches from side to side, and 53.5 inches from ground to roof. Curb weight was about 4,200 pounds, and the base price was roughly $4,600—more than twice that of the 1957 Ranchero. The Torino was discontinued in 1976, so the 1977 Ranchero had to borrow its facade from the Ford Elite.

Ford sold 508,355 hybrid half-tons from 1957 to 1979: 45,814 first-generation versions, 139,694 Falcon-based models, and 322,847 of the rest. Peak year was 1973, with 45,741 Rancheros hitting the road. Dearborn also marked the end of the Ranchero line in 1979 with a Limited Production version, a truly dressy concoction that came complete with an exclusive exterior plate engraved with the owner's initials.

Ford's first Ranchero was offered in two forms, a yeo-man standard model and upscale Custom rendition. Typically the Custom was treated to a more distinctive exterior, accomplished by adding the Custom 300 car's body-length trim spear. This trim, in turn, made it possible to order the "Style Tone" two-tone paint scheme.

1957 Ranchero

Wheelbase: 116 inches

Length: 203.5 inches

Width: 77 inches

Height: 58.7 inches

Weight: 3,520 pounds

Price: $2,098 for base model; $2,149 for Custom

Engine: 144-horsepower, 223-cubic-inch L-head inline six-cylinder, standard; 190-horsepower, 272-cubic-inch OHV V8, optional; 212-horsepower, 292-cubic-inch OHV V8, optional

Transmission: three-speed manual, standard; Ford-O-Matic automatic, optional

Production: 21,695 (included 15,277 Customs, 6,418 base models)

(Above) Originally born of Ford's two-door Ranch wagon, the 1957 Ranchero shared the station wagon line's tailgate and rear compartment sub-floor. Stampings unique to the Ranchero included the roof, upper cab panel (with exclusive rear window), double-walled cargo box, bed floor, and tailgate inner panel. With that tailgate down, total bed length measured about eight feet. Specified payload capacity was 1,190 pounds. Maximum gross vehicle weight (GVS) was 4,600 pounds.

(Right) These Sunburst full wheel covers were among the many car-line options also made available for Ford's first Ranchero.

The Ranchero's public introduction came on November 12, 1956, in Quitman, Georgia. Public relations officials that day presented one to Wesley Patrick, a celebrated Future Farmers of America "Star Farmer" then being honored. Young Patrick, however, wasn't impressed; he quickly traded his Ranchero for a new 1957 passenger car.

1957 Custom Ranchero Features
Bright metal cap molding around top of body and rear of cab
Bright metal full-length body side moldings
"Style Tone" two-tone paint option available (thanks to those side moldings)
"Style Tone" option featured 10 different colors matched w/Colonial White
Four upholstery colors offered with white vinyl facings and bolsters inside

(Above) Two V8s were available for the 1957 Ranchero, a 272-cubic-inch version and its 292-cube big brother, shown here. Output for this Y-block was 212 horsepower.

(Right) Like Ford's traditional half-ton pickups, the 1957 Ranchero came standard with small hubcaps.

Ford designers more or less simply cut the rear roof area away from a two-door station wagon to create the Ranchero in 1957. Ford built the Ranchero continuously up through 1979.

<u>"Ford's new Ranchero really does a day's work . . .</u>
. . . and does it in a style that pays business dividends. Because Ranchero, with its crisp modern lines, has a wonderful way of saying nice things about your company. Nice things like 'progressive,' 'up-to-date,' 'good to deal with.' That's why the Ranchero is excellent for any business—large or small—where customers' impressions count."

—*1957 Ford Ranchero brochure*

The base Ranchero in 1957 shared interior trimmings with the Ranch Wagon on which it was based. Upholstery shades were either tan/brown with tan vinyl bolsters or blue vinyl with white bolsters, depending on exterior paint choice.

Evidence of just what a great idea Ford's first Ranchero was came two years later when Chevrolet introduced its El Camino, an unabashed knock-off that both outsold and outlived its rival in the long run. The last El Camino was sold early in 1988.

After selling 21,695 Rancheros in 1957, Ford followed that up with only 9,950 in 1958. Production of the 1959 rendition (shown here) was 14,169. This was the last year for a full-sized Ranchero.

1959 Ranchero
Wheelbase: 118 inches
Length: 208 inches
Width: 76.6 inches
Height: 57.8 inches
Weight: 3,870 pounds
Base price: $2,312
Engine: 145-horsepower, 223-cid inline "Mileage Maker" six-cylinder, std.; 200-horsepower, 292-cid V8, optional; 225-horsepower, 332-cid V8 optional; 300-horsepower, 352-cid V8, optional
Transmission: three-speed manual, standard; Fordomatic and Cruise-O-Matic automatics, optional

Wheelbase for the first two Ranchero renditions was 116 inches. That measurement was stretched to 118 inches for 1959, resulting in a cargo box floor that was seven inches longer than before.

Interior appointments were shared by the Ranchero and Country Sedan/Country Squire station wagons in 1959. Ford's restyled instrument panel that year was a one-hit wonder—another redesign followed in 1960 for full-sized models.

Ford's 145-horsepower, 223-cubic-inch Mileage Maker six-cylinder (shown here) was one of four engines offered for the 1959 Ranchero. Three V8s also were available.

1960 Ranchero

Wheelbase: 109.5 inches

Length: 189 inches

Width: 70 inches

Height: 54.5 inches

Shipping weight: 2,435 pounds

Price: $1,882

Engine: 90-horsepower, 144-cid inline six-cylinder

Transmission: three-speed manual, standard; Fordomatic automatic, optional

Rolling on a 109.5-inch wheelbase, the 1960 Ranchero measured 19 inches shorter overall than its full-sized 1959 forerunner. Total production for 1960 was 21,027.

(Above) Downsizing from the full-sized Ford line to the new compact Falcon in 1960 meant trading a traditional full-sized frame for cost-conscious unit-body construction.

(Right)
Though based on the truly compact Falcon, the 1960 Ranchero still bragged of 31.6 cubic feet of cargo space in back in a bed that was six feet long. Advertised payload capacity was 800 pounds.

A Cobra Jet Ranchero GT was hot enough in 1971; bolting on a set of Magnum 500 five-spoke wheels warmed things up even further. Seen here are owner-preferred 15-inch Magnum 500s instead of the correct (for the Ranchero) 14-inch units.

1971 429 Cobra Jet V8
Type: overhead-valve 385-series big-block V8
Bore & stroke: 4.36 x 3.59 inches
Compression: 11.3:1
Induction: single 715-cfm four-barrel Rochester Quadrajet carburetor*
  * (ram-air Shaker hood scoop, optional)
Horsepower: 370 at 5,400 rpm
Torque: 450 lbs-ft at 3,400 rpm

Like the 428 Cobra Jet V8, the 429 CJ was rated the same, 370 horsepower with or without optional ram-air equipment. The 429 CJ was discontinued after 1971.

All of the Torino's sporty accoutrements, including bucket seats and a console with floor shifter, were again available for the Ranchero in 1971.

A full frame returned beneath the restyled Ranchero for 1972. Unitized body/frame construction had been the norm since the Ranchero was downsized into Falcon ranks in 1960.

1972 Ranchero GT
Wheelbase: 118 inches
Length: 215.7 inches
Width: 79 inches
Height: 53.1 inches
Shipping weight: 3,295 pounds
Base price: $2,850
Engine: 150-horsepower, 250-cid inline six-cylinder, standard.; 302-cid V8 standard on GT model
Transmission: three-speed manual, standard

Total Ranchero production for 1972 was 40,334, including 23,431 Gran Torino 500 models, 4,283 Gran Torino Squires, and 12,620 Gran Torino Sport GTs.

Optional goodies abounded for the 1972 Ranchero, including the Flight Bench Seat with fold-down center armrests. An impact-absorbing steering wheel (with padded hub), recessed door handles, and steel guard beams inside the doors were standard on the newly safety-conscious Ranchero.

While front-end styling for the 1977–'79 Ranchero mimicked the Ford Elite, body lines were borrowed from Mercury's Montego. Ford marked the end of the Ranchero line in 1979 with this Limited Production model. A vinyl roof, wire wheel covers, and extra body side trim were standard.

1977 Ranchero

Wheelbase: 118 inches

Length: 220.1 inches

Width: 79.6 inches

Height: 53.5 inches

Curb weight: 4,215 pounds

Base price: $4,618 (Ranchero 500), $4,971 (Ranchero Squire), $4,984 (Ranchero GT)

Available engines: 302-cubic-inch V8, 351-cubic-inch V8, 400-cubic-inch V8

Transmission: Select-Shift Cruise-O-Matic automatic

Production: 23,041

Whitewall tires and a choice between wire wheel covers on standard steel rims or Magnum 500 sport wheels were included in the Limited Production package. These 15-inch turbine-style wheels were also available on the Ford options list.

Vanity mirrors were standard inside the Limited Production Ranchero. Six-way power control was standard for the driver's seat, and also included in the deal was air conditioning, a tilt steering column, and the Sport Instrument Group. Completing the package was a gold-plate plaque personalized with the customer's initials.

Limited Production interiors in 1979 were done in Dark Red and featured upscale door panels borrowed from Mercury's XR-7 Cougar. The Thunderbird Heritage model donated its leather dashboard pad, rich carpeting, leather-wrapped steering wheel (with luxury horn ring), and cruise control. The two leather "lounge seats" also were similar to Thunderbird units but with headrests removed.

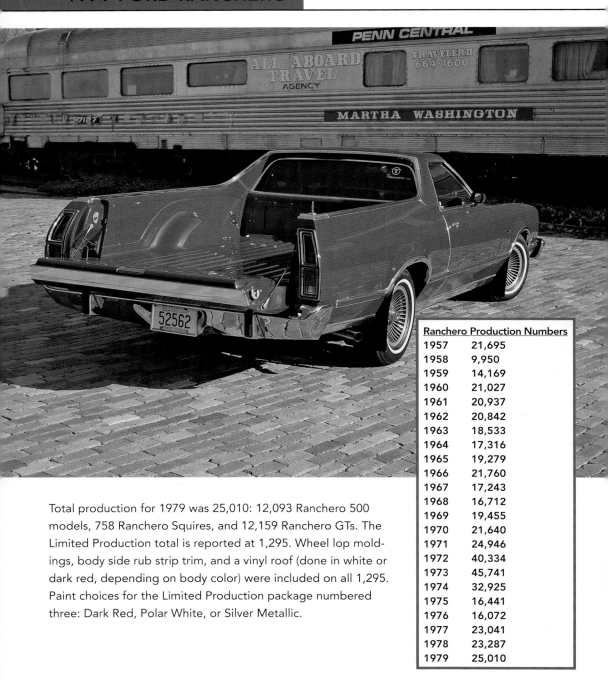

Total production for 1979 was 25,010: 12,093 Ranchero 500 models, 758 Ranchero Squires, and 12,159 Ranchero GTs. The Limited Production total is reported at 1,295. Wheel lop moldings, body side rub strip trim, and a vinyl roof (done in white or dark red, depending on body color) were included on all 1,295. Paint choices for the Limited Production package numbered three: Dark Red, Polar White, or Silver Metallic.

Ranchero Production Numbers	
1957	21,695
1958	9,950
1959	14,169
1960	21,027
1961	20,937
1962	20,842
1963	18,533
1964	17,316
1965	19,279
1966	21,760
1967	17,243
1968	16,712
1969	19,455
1970	21,640
1971	24,946
1972	40,334
1973	45,741
1974	32,925
1975	16,441
1976	16,072
1977	23,041
1978	23,287
1979	25,010

(Above) Only two Windsor-series small-block V8s were available for the 1979 Ranchero: one at 302 cubic inches, the other at 351. Both featured two-barrel carburetors.

(Right) Reportedly many Limited Production models were loaded down with extra features as parts bins were emptied out during the Ranchero phase-out process. The long list of options in this case includes a power-operated radio antenna.

Utility in Motion

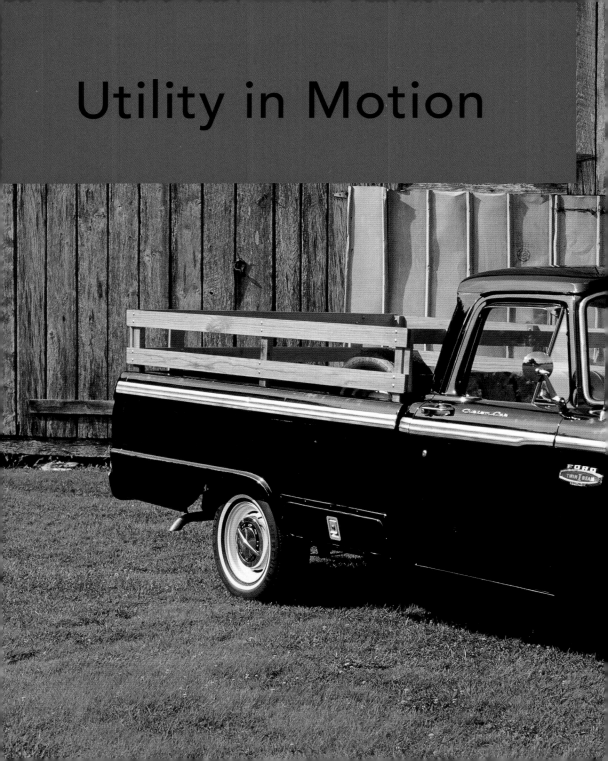

Chapter 6

Picking up the pace into the Seventies

Signs that Americans were changing the way they looked at the good ol' pickup were everywhere during the Sixties. No longer simply all work and no play, light-duty trucks soon started showing up more often with more of the comforts and conveniences car buyers already had begun taking for granted. Power steering and brakes, automatic transmissions, even air conditioning—these driver-friendly options and countless others gained popularity each year on the utility vehicle's side of the fence as this decade rolled onward and upward. More power, too, became more popular, with V8 installations outpacing their six-cylinder alternatives by the time the Seventies arrived.

Ford truck buyers, of course, had been familiar with V8 performance since 1932, far longer than any of their Dodge- and Chevy-loving friends. One year after Ford's first optional automatic transmission appeared, Henry's venerable flathead V8 finally was replaced by Dearborn's modern overhead-valve Y-block in 1954, just as Dodge was introducing an available V8 for its pickup line. Chevrolet's sensational small-block V8 then followed suit in 1955.

Adding those two extra cylinders wasn't done solely to help haul around extra tools. Pulling, say, a boat trailer with confidence was more like it. By the Sixties, reportedly two out of three pickups were serving double duty as both a work truck and a recreational vehicle, and Ford responded additionally to this trend with its ground-breaking Camper Special package. Introduced for 1965, this vacation-conscious option included extra cooling, a heavy-duty battery, and dual Western-style mirrors, all the better to take the entire family out roughing it in the great outdoors with relative ease. Hauling around the entire crew, either related to or employed by the owner, also was made easier by Ford's first four-door Crew Cab, unveiled in 1965 for the 3/4-ton F-250 and 1-ton F-350.

Image consciousness also gained prominence during the Sixties, demonstrated most plainly by Blue Oval buyers' growing preference for the trendy Styleside body, introduced in 1957, over the traditional, far less flashy stepside cargo box, called a Flareside in Ford parlance. Even more style and flair became available in 1965 by way of the new Ranger package, offered only for the Styleside pickup. According to Ford, this option was "designed to appeal to the luxury and sports-minded light truck operator." Bucket seats were included, as were classy carpeting, a cover panel for the gas tank, and appropriate "Ranger" ornamentation. A center console also was listed at additional cost. Another class act, the Explorer Special, appeared midyear in 1968.

Appearing as well were various variations on the Ford truck theme. Mimicking Chevrolet's forward-control Corvair 95 pickup in 1961 was Ford's Econoline, a unit-body utility vehicle offered in both van and pickup forms up through 1967. In 1966, Ford designers also copied their International-Harvester counterparts, matching I-H's little Scout, introduced for 1961, with the equally diminutive Bronco. Various styles were offered, including a pickup, prophetically labeled the Sport Utility.

From a mechanical perspective, the biggest news made during this decade involved the truck's dirty side, where Ford's highly publicized Twin I-Beam front suspension debuted for 1965. Ever-present ad guys touted this double swing-axle layout as the next great thing in pickup design, even though it was far from cutting edge, especially so considering Chevrolet had been offering car-like short-arm/long-arm (SLA) independent front suspension since 1960. Whatever the case, those rugged Twin I-Beams continued handling rough terrain beneath an F-series Ford's front end until finally replaced by modern SLA underpinnings in 1997.

Ford's unit-body Econoline models debuted for 1961 in (left to right) van, station bus, and pickup forms. The Econoline legacy ended in 1967.

Ford designers went one step beyond in 1961 with a Styleside makeover that featured an integral cab/bed body. This arrangement was available only for the F-100 and F-250. The big F-350 was limited to the traditional Flareside body.

1961 F-100
Wheelbase: 114 inches
Length: 189.1 inches (short bed)
Height: 75.5 inches
Weight: 3,129 pounds (w/six-cylinder)
Price: $1,935.73 (base Styleside w/six-cylinder engine)
Standard engine: 135-horsepower, 223-cubic-inch six-cylinder
Optional engine: 160-horsepower, 292-cubic-inch V8
Standard transmission: three-speed manual (four-speed, overdrive, and automatic, all optional)
Production: 62,410 (Styleside)

118

(Above) Ford's 223-cubic-inch inline six-cylinder was standard in 1961. A 292-cubic-inch V8 was optional.

(Left) A column-shifted three-speed manual transmission was standard for the 1961 F-100. Overdrive, a four-speed manual, and Fordomatic automatic were options.

A difficult engineering proposition from the outset due to the torsional stresses inherent in the basic pickup layout, Ford's integral body lasted only three years before the F-100 was again offered with a conventional cargo box bolted on behind a stand-alone cab. Only recently has Detroit dared to try mating the two again.

F-100 Cab Dimensional Comparison

	1960	1961
Windshield size	1,020 sq. inches	1,247 sq. inches
Rear window size	407 sq. inches	600 sq. inches
Seat width	56.75 inches	56.75 inches
Hip room	63.12 inches	63.42 inches
Door height	43.38 inches	42 inches
Door width	37 inches	37.48 inches

223 CUBIC INCHES

HORSEPOWER 135

FOR SERVICE INSTRUCTIONS
SEE OPERATOR'S MANUAL

HOLLEY

Ford's overhead-valve six-cylinder made its 135 maximum horsepower at 4,000 rpm. Compression was 8.4:1.

A rather flashy new grille set the 1965 F-100 apart from its 1964 forerunner. Notice the appropriate hood badge on this V8-equipped model.

1965 F-100

Wheelbase: 115 inches (short bed)

Weight: 3,225 pounds

Price: $2,018 (base Styleside w/eight-foot box and six-cylinder engine)

Standard engine: 150-horsepower, 249-cubic-inch inline six-cylinder

Optional engines: 170-horsepower, 300-cubic-inch inline six-cylinder; 208-horsepower, 352-cubic-inch V8

Standard transmission: three-speed manual

Production: 178,571 (Styleside); 34,184 (Flareside)

Inexpensive floormats and seat coverings were still typical inside most pickups in 1965. Also notice the absent instrumentation in the dash.

Ford's 352-cubic-inch FE-series V8 was an option for the F-100 half-ton in 1965. Compression was 8.9:1.

Ford's Styleside pickups went back to conventional separate cab and cargo box construction in 1964. The bumper and tailgate trim on this 1965 F-100 are owner-installed customizations.

1965 F-100 Engines

	Standard six-cylinder	Optional six-cylinder	Optional V8
Bore & stroke	4.0 x 3.18 inches	4.0 x 3.98 inches	4.0 x 3.50 inches
Displacement	249 cubic inches	300 cubic inches	352 cubic inches
Compression	9.2:1	8.0:1	8.9:1
Carburetor	one-barrel	one-barrel	two-barrel
Horsepower	150 at 4,000 rpm	170 at 3,600 rpm	208 at 4,400 rpm
Torque	234 at 2,200 rpm	293 at 2,400 rpm	315 at 2,400 rpm

Twin I-Beam front suspension debuted in 1965 and remained in place beneath an F-series pickup's nose until 1997.

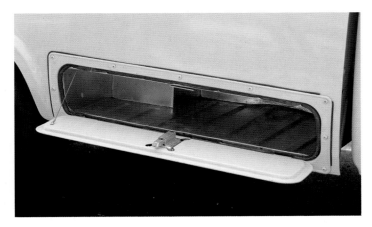

An optional passenger-side toolbox could've been added to the F-100 cargo box in 1965.

Ford's old solid-beam axle and leaf springs were replaced in 1965 by two long swing axles and coils springs to help each front wheel roll independently over road jars and bumps. *Ford brochure*

Yet another new grille appeared for the F-100 in 1966. Deluxe two-tone paint with bright trim was a $54 option that year.

1966 F-100 Base Prices

	Flareside	Styleside
115-inch wheelbase	$2,069	$2,085
129-inch wheelbase	$2,105	$2,121

Ford built 224,497 Styleside pickups for 1966, compared to 26,491 Flaresides.

Small dog-dish hubcaps were again standard for an F-series pickup in 1966.

An automatic transmission and underdash air conditioner were optional for the F-100 in 1966. The upholstery is an owner-added preference.

The wheelbase for a long-bed F-100 in 1966 was 129 inches, compared to 115 for its short-bed counterpart.

Did we goof by making FORD No. I in Pickup ride?

That is, are we risking our pickup's hard-earned reputation for ruggedness by giving it the smoothest ride going?

Not at all. Twin-I-Beam suspension is our insurance.

It works like this . . . each front wheel has its own axle—a forged steel I-beam, like big truck I-beams. They work independently, so that shocks at one wheel don't get passed to the other. Or to the driver.

Ford also puts husky I-beam radius rods up front to hold wheel alignment and reduce tire wear.

Together, they make an independent suspension that no other pickup can match for smoothness . . . toughness.

Engines are smoother, too. Two big new, seven-main-bearing Sixes have such performance, we had to develop a new V-8 to stay ahead of them.

So are we worried? Not when our biggest concern is building enough to meet the demand. So far this year our sales are up eighteen percent.

Come on in and check us out. Action-test a new Ford today.

FORD/66

Dearborn engineers in 1965 made news with their highly publicized Twin I-Beam front suspension, which reportedly helped an F-100 roll over bumps and jolts like no truck before. *1966 Ford advertisement*

Selected 1966 F-100 Options	
Custom Cab package	$96
Camper Special package (for 129-inch wheelbase only)	$58
Regular two-tone paint	$16.50
Deluxe two-tone paint (for Styleside models only)	$54
Ranger package w/bucket seats (Custom Cab required)	$97
Power steering (not available with four-wheel-drive)	$108
Stowage compartment, left or right side	$10.50
Stowage compartment, both left and right side	$21
Cruise-O-Matic automatic transmission	$212.50

Compact pickups from Japan first began invading American shores in 1958, inspiring International-Harvester to roll out its little Scout in 1961. Ford then responded with its first Bronco five years later. Four-wheel drive was standard.

1966 Bronco roadster
Wheelbase: 92 inches
Length: 152.1 inches
Height: 69.2 inches
Curb Weight: 3,107 pounds
Price: $2,480
Engine: 105-horsepower, 170-cubic-inch inline six-cylinder
Transmission: three-speed manual
Production: 4,090

A 170-cubic-inch inline six-cylinder engine was standard beneath the 1966 Bronco's hood.
Output was 105 horsepower.

The Ranger package was priced at $238.20 in 1970. It was available only for Styleside models.

1970 F-100 Base Prices		
	Custom Flareside	*Custom Styleside*
115-inch wheelbase	$2,509.24	$2,548.24
131-inch wheelbase	$2,548.24	$2,584.75
115-inch wheelbase 4x4	$3,155.49	$3,129.24
131-inch wheelbase 4x4	$3,192.24	$3,231.24

(Left) Deluxe wheel covers were included on Ranger models in 1970.

(Below) Woodtone interior trim was part of the Ranger deal in 1970. Notice the heavy-duty floor shifter for the optional four-speed manual transmission.

A decorative tailgate panel was part of the Ranger package in 1970, as were various bits of bright trim.

Introduced as an optional package for the 1965 Styleside, the Ranger became the F-series pickup's supremely trimmed model in 1967. The Ranger XLT then came along to top things off in 1970.

Selected 1970 F-100 Options	
Air conditioning	$406.80
SelectShift Cruise-O-Matic automatic transmission (6-cyl.)	$222.70
SelectShift Cruise-O-Matic automatic transmission (V8)	$231.70
Power steering	$127.50
Vacuum power brake booster	$45.30
300-cid six-cylinder engine	$90.10
302-cid V8 (included heavy-duty springs)	$90.10
360-cid V8 (included heavy-duty springs)	$127.50
390-cid V8 (not available w/4x4)	$263.90
Ranger package (Styleside)	$238.20
Ranger XLT package (Styleside)	$347.50

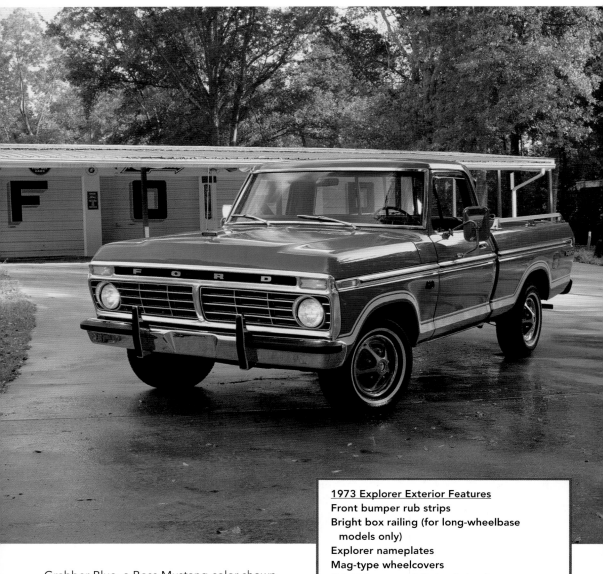

1973 Explorer Exterior Features
Front bumper rub strips
Bright box railing (for long-wheelbase
  models only)
Explorer nameplates
Mag-type wheelcovers
Bright low-mount Swing-Lok mirrors
Bright drip moldings
Bright windshield moldings
Body side tape stripes
Bright front bumper guards

Grabber Blue, a Boss Mustang color shown here, and Explorer Green were initially listed as available finishes for Explorer Specials. But other shades also were available by special order.

Various Explorer packages were offered during the early Seventies, and some of these deals included mag-type deluxe wheelcovers.

The Explorer Special package appeared midyear in 1968. Today the badge is best known for its leading role in SUV ranks.

Extra bright trim and ornamental cargo box rails, also chromed, were included in the Explorer Special package, as were bodyside tape stripes.

1973 F-100 Paint Choices

Raven Black	Wind Blue	Pure White
Wimbledon White	Chrome Yellow	Seapine Green
Winter Green	Limestone Green	Mallard Green
Sequoia Brown Metallic	Midnight Blue Metallic	Candyapple Red
Durango Tan	Royal Blue	Tampico Yellow

1973 Explorer Package Choices: Burnt Orange, Grabber Blue, Bright Lime

(Left) Explorer interior appointments complemented their exterior finishes. The Explorer Special package also included power steering, power brakes, and SelectShift automatic transmission.

(Below) The 390-cubic-inch big-block was one of three available V8s in 1973; 360-cid and 302-cid engines also were available. The 390 produced 189 horsepower.

Thirty Years and Counting

Chapter 7

Ford remains number one

Thirty years is a long time in anyone's book, certainly so as far as Detroit is concerned. In a town where big news in the morning is often old news by day's end, staying on top of things is not an easy task, especially now that so much more competition for headlines comes from other not-so-familiar burgs halfway around the world. The truck tale's front page, formerly dominated by the Big Three, is presently shared by the likes of Toyota, Honda, and Nissan, with the latter's west-side story dating back 50 years as these words come off the press. Yet we still have Ford's F-series standing tall and true as America's best-selling pickup, just as it has since 1977.

Few truck watchers today seem to remember that it was Chevrolet who led the way for 30 years. After spending so many years working their way back to the top, Ford people weren't about to stand by and watch the former leader run away and hide again. Sure, Chevy did retake the lead a time or two during the Seventies. But it was the Dearborn gang who emerged from the decade with a stranglehold on the brass ring they've yet to release.

Countless trendsetting upgrades and a milestone or two have helped Ford stay out in front over this long haul. Notable during the Seventies was the new F-150, introduced for 1975 as a "heavy half-ton" alternative to the wildly popular F-100, which in 1973 had become America's third best-selling vehicle behind only Chevrolet and Ford's full-sized passenger-car lines. Nicely restyled that year, the latest, greatest F-100 represented, in the words of Ford general manager John Naughton, "a new generation of better ideas." But too bad the bulb that had burned so brightly since 1953 was soon on its way out. F-150 popularity quickly took over, leaving the good ol' F-100 fading from the limelight. Ford's heavy half-ton then became the company's base pickup in 1984 after the F-100 quietly retired.

Dearborn designers in 1980 bragged of building the first new truck for the next decade, a sharp-edged, boxy pickup that successfully stuck around for a dozen years. Those crisp corners were rounded off somewhat in 1987, then a truly aerodynamic restyle appeared for 1992. Also new during the Eighties was a reborn Ranger, a downsized package created to help stave off the aforementioned Japanese invasion, which had first landed, however humbly, in California late in 1958.

New at a Los Angeles import auto show that December was a truly tiny pickup from Nissan's alter-ego, Datsun. A quaint curiosity at first, Datsun's little truck was followed equally quietly in 1964 by another pint-sized hauler from Toyota, and it was shove following push from there. Compact trucks began gaining favor during the Seventies, with both Nissan and Toyota selling more than 100,000 a year in America by 1979.

Ford did respond, somewhat, with its Econoline in 1961 and Bronco in 1966 but didn't actually confront the newcomers from Nippon directly until 1972, and only then by sleeping with the enemy. Ford hooked up with Japan's Mazda firm that year to help produce a certified compact called Courier. At the same time, Chevrolet teamed up with Isuzu to create its little LUV, which was short for Light Utility Vehicle. With Detroit now contributing full-force to the tally, market-wide compact truck sales for 1972 more than doubled the annual total seen just two years before. And by 1986, Americans were buying more compacts than full-sized models. Traditional pickups regained majority status two years later, but their smaller running mates have remained a viable alternative ever since.

Introduced in 1982 as a 1983 model, Ford's downsized Ranger countered Chevrolet's new S-10, another compact half-ton intended to prove that it was better to buy American. Four-cylinder power was standard for the 1982 Ranger, and both two-wheel- and four-wheel-drive versions were offered. Four years later, the latter Ranger rendition was named "4x4 of the Year" by *4-Wheel and Off-Road* magazine.

Back in the mainstream, Ford's F-series trucks were treated to another major makeover in the Nineties. Introduced with much hoopla in January 1996, the 1997 F-150 featured an aerodynamic restyle that critics either loved or hated. Buyers, however, fit mostly into the former class because demand immediately overwhelmed supply. Attractions included the all-new Triton-series modular engines, which traded traditional pushrods for cutting-edge overhead-cam construction. Four-wheel disc brakes were standard, too, for the first time in pickup history. Last but certainly not least, the 1997 F-150 also finally brought an end to the Twin I-Beam legacy.

Not to rest on their laurels, Ford truck designers came back with yet another next-generation F-series pickup in 2004. "Our vision was to forge a new direction for the market, building decisively on Ford's Tough Truck heritage and creating a product that would alter the expectations of pickup customers," explained Ford's North American Product Development Vice President Chris Theodore. A deeper cargo box, a larger cab with extra rear seat room and enhanced safety features, and a fully boxed frame that measured nine times more torsionally stiff than its forerunner represented just a few of the many notable upgrades.

Along with an available 5.4-liter, 3-valve Triton (that made 300 horsepower), all this newness also was wrapped up in an aggressively restyled shell that left little doubt about which truck was still number one around Detroit. "The [2004] F-150 exudes the confidence of a leader," bragged Ford Design Vice President J. Mays. "It reaches back to the roots of the Ford F-series tradition to communicate a tough, visual strength with boldness and honesty."

Here's to another 30 years out in front.

Initially only offered in 4x2 standard cab form in 1993, Ranger Splash availability increased the following year to include both standard cab and SuperCab models with either conventional two-wheel-drive or a 4x4 drivetrain. A 1995 4x4 Ranger Splash SuperCab appears here.

<u>1995 Ranger Splash Supercab</u>
Wheelbase: 135.2 inches
Curb weight: 3,237 pounds
Price: $19,446
Standard engine: 4.0-liter EFI V6
Transmission: four-speed automatic-overdrive
Production: 215,416 (total for all Ranger models)

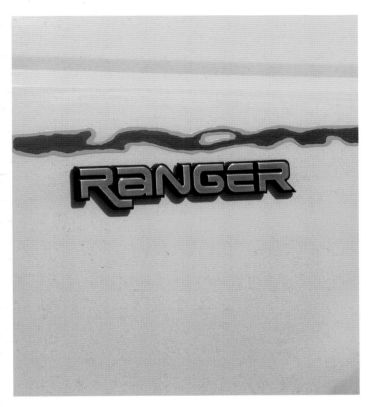

First used in 1967 to denote a dress-up package for Ford's full-sized F-series pickups, the Ranger nameplate was reaffixed to the company's new compact truck 15 years later. The downsized Ranger was introduced in 1982 (as a 1983 model) to counter Chevrolet's little S-10.

America's best-selling compact pickup was extensively restyled for 1993, and the Splash rendition debuted midyear to enhance the attraction further. In 1995 the Splash package added $598 to the $19,466 base price of a Ranger 4x4 SuperCab.

A Flareside cargo box was the most notable Splash feature. Also included in the package were a sliding rear window and a monochromatic finish adorned with humble, yet still flashy, graphics.

1995 Ranger Model/Series Availability

Trim Package	Regular cab 4x2 SWB	Regular cab 4x4 SWB	Regular cab 4x2 LWB	Regular cab 4x4 LWB	SuperCab 4x2/4x4
XL	X	X	X	X	X
XL Sport	X	X	X	X	n/a
Splash	X	X	n/a	n/a	X
XLT	X	X	X	X	X
STX (4x4 only)	n/a	X	n/a	X	X

"X" signifies that trim package is available with that particular platform
SWB=short wheelbase; LWB=long wheelbase

(Above) A 2.3-liter four-cylinder was the standard engine for the Ranger Splash in 1995. Two V6s were optional, a 145-horsepower 3.0-liter version and this 4.0-liter, rated at 160 horsepower.

(Left) A cloth 60/40 split bench seat was a no-cost Ranger Splash option in 1995. Other options appearing here include a CD changer, power windows and locks, air conditioning, cruise control, and tilt steering wheel.

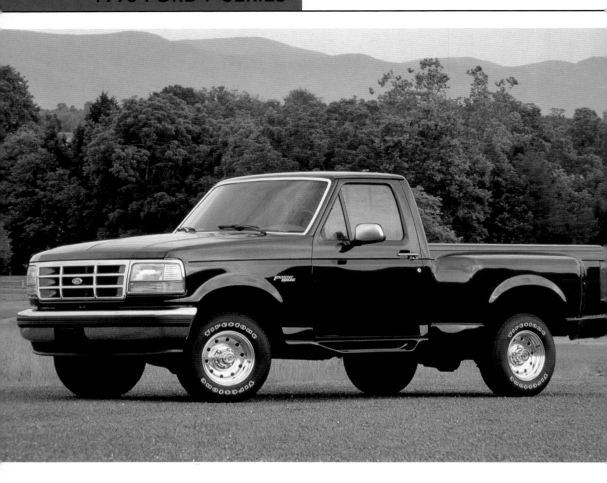

Available F-150 models for 1995 included regular and SuperCab bodies backed by either a Flareside (shown here) or Styleside cargo box. Available trim packages included the standard Special, XL, XLT, and the new Eddie Bauer edition.

1980 F-100
Wheelbase: 117 inches
Weight: 3,324 pounds
Price: $5,549
Standard engine: 300-cubic-inch inline six-cylinder (73 percent of 1980 F-100s featured this engine)
Transmission: three-speed manual
Production: 133,590 (F-150 production for 1980 was 173,050)

(Above) Like the regular-cab model, the F-150 SuperCab came in both standard rear-wheel-drive and 4x4 forms in 1995. SuperCabs were available in two wheelbases, 139 and 155 inches.

(Below) Three bodies were offered for the big 1-ton F-350 pickup in 1995: regular, SuperCab, and Crew Cab, all backed only by the Styleside cargo box. The F-350 also was offered in 4x2 and 4x4 forms and could have been fitted with "dualie" wheels in back.

"Built Ford Tough" took on all-new meaning in 1997, since the redesigned F-150 was the most rugged yet. "This truck is both a workhorse and a show horse," bragged Ross Roberts, Ford Motor Company vice president and Ford Division general manager.

<u>1997 F-150 SuperCab</u>
Wheelbase: 138.8 inches
Weight: 4,200 pounds
Price: $23,885
Standard engine: 5.4-liter EFI SOHC V8 (optional)
Transmission: four-speed automatic-overdrive
Production: 710,301 (all F-150 models for extended 1996–'97 run)

(Above) Ford Motor Company's 1997 truck lineup: Ranger, Mercury Mountaineer, Ranger Splash, Explorer, Expedition, F-150 Flareside, and F-150 Styleside.

(Below) More than five million miles' worth of hard testing went by before the Blue-Oval boys rolled out their totally new F-150 for 1997. "Using our field experience plus durability and other test procedures, we did what was necessary to make the truck Ford tough," said vehicle engineering manager Bob Himes.

Ford's restyled, redesigned 1997 F-150 was bigger inside and out compared to its predecessor and delivered the highest V8 payload capacity in its class. "Ford's new F-150 takes the concept of the full-size pickup to a new level in terms of features and functional attributes," added Ford Motor Company exec Ross Roberts.

F-series Milestones	
January 16, 1948	"Bonus Built" F-series truck introduced
F-100 replaced F-1	
1959	First factory-complete 4x4 offered
1965	Twin I-Beam front suspension introduced
1974	SuperCab model introduced
F-150 model introduced	
1978	F-series sales hit 864,000, a new record
1980	Diesel power debuted in pickup lineup
1987	Ford trucks first to offer rear-wheel ABS
1995	F-series surpasses Volkswagen Beetle as world's all-time best-selling vehicle
January 16, 1998	50th anniversary celebration

(Left) Ford introduced a heavy-duty half-ton pickup, the F-150, in 1975. Both the traditional F-100 and F-150 rolled on together until the former retired at the end of 1983. The F-150 has been Ford's sole light truck offering ever since.

(Below) New, too, for 1997 were Ford's Triton-series modular engines, which traded traditional pushrods for cutting-edge overhead-cam construction. First in the Triton lineup was a 4.2-liter V8, standard for all but Ford's 4x4 SuperCab trucks. Optional were the 4.6- and 5.4-liter (shown here) Triton V8s.

Wheelbase for the 1997 F-150 4x2 Flareside SuperCab was 119.9 inches. Overall length was 224.5 inches. This 1997 F-150 is adorned with the optional Lariat package, which among other things included lower bodyside two-tone paint.

"Ford is the leading manufacturer of trucks worldwide, and we're very proud of the success of the F-series family. Ford's new F-150 takes the concept of the full-size pickup to a new level in terms of features and functional attributes, while continuing to combine the legendary tough and rugged performance our customers expect."

—*Ford Motor Company vice president and Ford Division general manager Ross Roberts on the redesigned 1997 F-150*

(Left) The 1997 SuperCab established a new industry trend, becoming the first pickup to offer a standard third door. The six-way power driver's seat seen inside this SuperCab was included as part of the Lariat package.

(Below) Ford celebrated 50 years of F-series pickups in 1998, touring the auto show circuit that year with both its newest F-150 and a wonderfully restored 1948 F-1. The two pause here in Atlanta.

In 1998 Ford rolled out its NASCAR Edition F-150 to help mark the 50th anniversaries of both the NASCAR stock-car circuit and the F-series pickup line. Black paint, an XLT mesh grille, a Roush front air dam, and official exterior graphics were standard for all 3,000 NASCAR Edition trucks built that year. The bug screen seen here is an owner-added item.

1998 NASCAR Edition F-150
Model: 4x2 regular-cab Styleside (with special mesh grille, NASCAR graphics, and Roush front air dam)
Wheelbase: 120 inches
Price: NASCAR Edition package added $3,990 to the 1998 F-150 base price ($15,865)
Engine: standard F-150 4.6-liter V8 with dual Roush stainless-steel exhaust tips (exiting on passenger side)
Transmission: choice between five-speed manual or automatic
Axle ratio: 3.73:1
Tires: Goodyear A/S with yellow lettering
Wheels: black-painted 16x7 10-spoke aluminum
Production: 3,000, all painted black with grey interiors

All NASCAR Edition F-150s were 4x2, regular-cab, short-box models. Most were sold in Ford's southeast regions—understandably so considering that's were NASCAR racing remains king. The NASCAR package added $3,990 to this truck's $15,865 bottom line.

Goodyear tires with yellow lettering and 16x7 10-spoke aluminum wheels, also done in black, were included in the NASCAR Edition deal. The suspension also was lowered an inch.

Ford's 1999 Super Duty SuperCab was the first truck in its class (8,500-pound gross vehicle weight and up) to feature four doors as standard equipment. "We believe the standard fourth door serves both commercial- and recreational-use customers," said Super Duty chief program engineer Dave Breedlove. "It allows commercial buyers to use both doors for easy access of people and cargo, or it allows personal-use customers the choice to use only the passenger-side rear door for their kids and pets."

"With everything we've done to enhance the Super Duty F-series lineup, we're pleased to be able to keep prices at levels that make these great new trucks an even better value for our customers. Our new Super Duty F-series lineup offers truck customers everything they've come to expect from Ford and more. We now have the most comprehensive range of models to meet the demands of the full-size market—the most diverse of all vehicle segments."

—Ford Motor Company vice president and Ford Division general manager Ross Roberts on the 1999 Super Duty

The Super Duty lineup was increased for 1999 to include F-250, F-350, F-450, and F-550 models. F-350 Super Duty trucks were available that year in both 4x2 and 4x4 forms with regular cabs, SuperCabs, or Crew Cabs. Single rear wheels and duals also were available.

Ford's new Super Duty pickups for 1999 (back), though big and burly, still offered more comforts of home than a garden-variety F-150 half-ton did in 1960.

Ford and Harley-Davison announced a partnership to develop specialty vehicles together in March 1999. The bad-and-black 2000 H-D F-150 then followed. A four-door SuperCab model in 2001, this special-edition pickup next appeared in Super Crew form (shown here) in 2003.

As fate would have it, both the Ford Motor Company and Harley-Davidson marked their 100th anniversaries in 2003.

Full instrumentation, leather appointments, front and rear consoles, and four captain's chairs were standard inside the 2003 Harley-Davison F-150.

2003 Harley-Davidson F-150 Super Crew
Wheelbase: 138.5 inches
Wheels: 20-inch chromed five-spoke
Price: $37,295
Standard engine: 5.4-liter supercharged SOHC V8
Advertised output: 340 horsepower
Transmission: four-speed automatic-overdrive
Production: 12,000 planned

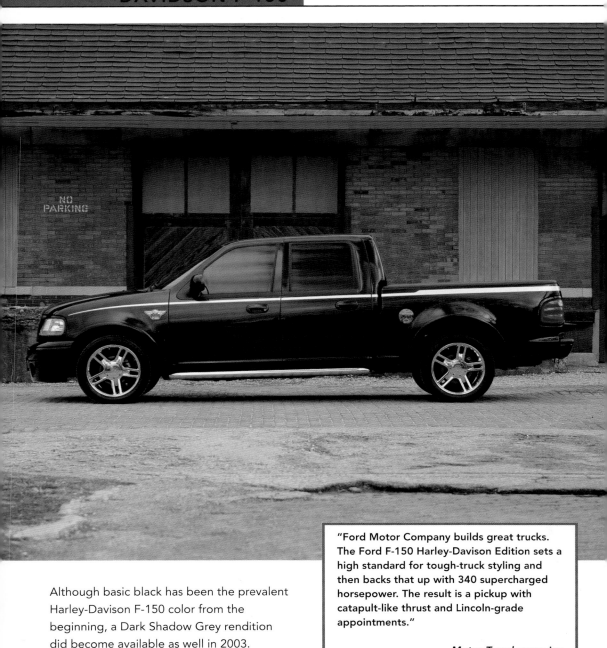

Although basic black has been the prevalent Harley-Davison F-150 color from the beginning, a Dark Shadow Grey rendition did become available as well in 2003.

"Ford Motor Company builds great trucks. The Ford F-150 Harley-Davison Edition sets a high standard for tough-truck styling and then backs that up with 340 supercharged horsepower. The result is a pickup with catapult-like thrust and Lincoln-grade appointments."

Motor Trend magazine

(Left) Big, bright, 20-inch chrome wheels were included as part of the Harley-Davidson special-edition package in 2003.

(Below) A detuned version of the SVT Lightning's supercharged 5.4-liter V8 was standard for the Harley-Davidson F-150 in 2003. Output in the H-D F-150's case was 340 horsepower.

Ford's sales leader was seriously revamped again for 2004. Improvements included a stiffened frame, increased power, a refined ride, and a more sumptuous cockpit. "I believe the sophistication and craftsmanship of its interior design is truly a benchmark achievement for this class of vehicle," claimed Ford Design vice president J. Mays. A 2006 F-150 appears here. *Photo courtesy of Ford Motor Company*

<u>2004 F-150 SuperCab</u>

Wheelbase: 144.4 inches

Weight: 5,421 pounds

Base price: $26,720

Standard engine: 4.6-liter Triton V6 or 5.4-liter Triton V8

Advertised output: 231 horsepower (V6); 300 horsepower (V8)

Brakes: four-wheel vented discs (13-inch rotors in front, 13.7 in back)

Transmission: four-speed automatic-overdrive

After moving up into the F-250 and F-350 Super Duty ranks in 2004, the H-D pickup reappeared as a half-ton F-150 model in 2006. Simply called the "boldest Harley-Davidson F-150 ever" by Ford president Steve Lyons, the '06 rendition featured available all-wheel drive, 22-inch polished aluminum wheels, and a "menacing monotone black exterior."

Ford's Steve Lyons claimed that the 2006 H-D F-150 SuperCab interior would "take your breath away." Rich leather, various chrome highlights, and high-gloss Piano Black treatments were standard, as were those ever-present captain's chairs. *Photo courtesy of Ford Motor Company*

As if its intimidating size didn't make it stand out enough, the 2007 Super Duty F-250 also was adorned with a huge chrome grille. This fully loaded 4x4 Lariat model also shows off the optional King Ranch package.

2007 F-250 Super Duty King Ranch
Wheelbase: 141.8 inches (with SuperCab)
Overall length: 231.8 inches (with SuperCab)
Base price: $37,980
Engine: 6.4-liter, four-valve turbo diesel V8 (optional)
Transmission: six-speed manual, standard; five-speed Torqshift automatic, optional
Brakes: four-wheel discs w/ABS

(Left) The Lariat rendition was the flagship of the Super Duty line in 2007. The base model was the XL, followed by the XLT. Among other things, the Lariat package included fog lights, alloy wheels, leather interior appointments, and a trip computer. King Ranch editions included a power sliding rear window, two-tone paint, painted alloy wheels, and illuminated cab steps.

(Below) Super Duty trucks featured three available engines in 2007: a 5.4-liter, 3-valve Triton V8; 6.8-liter, 3-valve Triton V10; and 6.4-liter, 4-valve turbo diesel V8. Output for the intercooled turbo diesel (shown here) was 300 horsepower. Compression was 9.8:1.

This Super Duty's clever tailgate features an easy-to-use step and hand-grip bar to make access up into its mile-high cargo box a cinch, even for height-challenged users.

Available 2007 Super Duty Engines			
Type	*Triton V8*	*Triton V10*	*Turbo Diesel V8*
Displacement	5.4 liters	6.8 liters	6.4 liters
Cylinder heads	aluminum	aluminum	cast-iron
Cylinder block	cast-iron	cast-iron	cast-iron
Valvetrain	SOHC 3-valve	SOHC 3-valve	OHV 4-valve
Fuel delivery	SEFI	SEFI	intercooled, dual-stage turbochargers, EFI
Horsepower	300 at 5,000 rpm	362 at 4,750 rpm	350 at 3,000 rpm
Compression	9.8:1	9.2:1	16.7:1
SEFI: sequential electronic fuel injection		*EFI: electronic fuel injection*	

The 2007 King Ranch leather-rich interior came standard with quad captain's chairs (the fronts were heated), front and rear consoles, and special trim. An automatic transmission was mandated.

Appropriate embossment on the King Ranch interior's seats also was part of the package.

Hot Rod Haulers

Chapter 8

SVT Lighting, 1993–2004

Once upon a time, a pickup's life was all work, no play. Then along came Chevrolet's Cameo Carrier in 1955 to prove that light trucks also could operate alongside cars on the classy side of the fence. More and more comforts of home began showing up in utility vehicles as the Sixties progressed, and before you knew it the barrier between automobile and truck had all but vanished.

Prestige and pizzazz are prime pickup selling points today because most buyers expect their cargo-carrying rides to look and act every bit as cool as their automotive counterparts. Furthermore, some customers even prefer their pickups to perform as well as Detroit's latest, greatest muscle cars. For these leadfoots, the Big Three have rolled out various hot rod haulers in recent years, the biggest, baddest being Dodge's outrageous 500-horsepower SRT-10, introduced for 2004 with the Viper's venomous V-10 beneath its bulging hood. In February 2004, the SRT-10 was recognized as the "World's Fastest Production Pickup Truck," according to *The Guinness Book of World Records*, this after running 154 mph on a test track.

That record previously belonged to a Ford, but only briefly. On August 13, 2003, a stone-stock F-150 reached 147.7 mph at the company's proving grounds in Romeo, Michigan. Not just any F-150, this particular half-ton came by way of Dearborn's Special Vehicle Team, a group dedicated to "apply the best available resources, both from inside and outside Ford, to explore new ways of creating and marketing high-performance vehicles." Founded in 1991, SVT is best known for its hot-to-trot Cobra Mustang, built from 1993 to 2004. The SVT touch also showed up on the Contour (1998–2000), the Focus (2002–2004), and the exotic GT supercar (2005–2006). Presently the SVT badge is worn by the 2007 Shelby GT500, even though the organization itself was essentially dissolved a few years ago.

Ford's first SVT Cobra debuted at the Chicago Auto Show in February 1992 along with another high-performance vehicle, the Lightning pickup. Unlike the Cobra, which was built by another newly formed division, Special Vehicle Engineering, the SVT Lightning was the work of Ford Truck Operations, which had been working independently on its own performance product while the Special Vehicle Team and its SVE support group were busy organizing themselves. Once SVT people got wind of the Lightning project, they opted to pair it up with the Cobra Mustang. Both then went on sale in February 1993.

Power came from a 5.8-liter (351-cubic-inch) V8 that used various GT-40 components to produce 240 healthy horses. Standard equipment behind those ponies included a four-speed automatic transmission and 4.10:1 gears. Typical performance numbers equaled 0–60 in 7.2 seconds, the quarter-mile in a tad more than 15 seconds. According to a 1994 SVT release, this hot rod F-150 more or less represented "a Mustang GT with a cargo bed instead of a backseat."

SVT Lightning production rolled on with few changes up through 1995 before temporarily shutting down. It then returned like a bolt out of the blue for 1999, this time armed with 360 horsepower. Delivering those horses was a supercharged, 5.4-liter, single-overhead-cam (SOHC) Triton V8. According to SVT tests, quarter-mile performance was 14.6 seconds at 97 mph.

On the outside was a more prominent image now based on the F-150 Flareside body instead of the Styleside package used by the first-generation Lightning. Up front was a unique front fascia incorporating round driving lights akin to the Cobra Mustang. Side-exit exhausts complemented things on the passenger's side.

Only minor updates marked the 2000 Lightning's arrival. But then the SVT folks really got cooking. "The 2001 SVT Lightning gives owners everything they have learned to love, but more of it," explained SVT chief engineer John Coletti. "It's the most powerful, best-handling one we've yet produced, and some dramatic design changes make this model instantly recognizable. There'll be no mistaking it from previous SVT Lightning models, and now it's even more strongly differentiated from the standard F-150."

A freshened front fascia, new wheels, and trendy crystalline lenses for both head- and taillamps weren't the only things setting the 2001 SVT Lightning apart from its forerunners. Twenty more supercharged horses were now standard thanks to a few enlarged pieces (mass airflow meter and air intake opening) and a higher-flow intake manifold. Performance, in turn, improved to 5.8 seconds for the 0–60 run, 13.9 ticks for the quarter-mile. Top end was listed at 142 unofficial miles per hour in 2001. That official 147-mph run then came two years later, to the delight of Ford truck fans across the land.

"We're proud to have certification from Guinness World Records," said SVT marketing and sales manager Tom Scarpello in August 2003. "It is a well-deserved record for the engineering team, and overdue confirmation to all the Lightning owners out there who have known for years that they drive the fastest truck on the planet."

SVT Lightning production continued into 2004 before coming to a halt. A bodacious next-generation Lightning concept vehicle featuring 500 horsepower appeared that year, but rumors are all that now remain of the super-duper F-150 that once rode atop the world.

Chevrolet's Cameo Carrier, built from 1955 to 1958, laid the groundwork for today's playtoy pickups. It was by no means a muscle machine, but it did represent a marked departure from the all-work/no-play trucks that came before. Its classy cargo box allowed it to fit in relatively well in polite society, and it also inspired Ford's F-100 Styleside body, introduced for 1957.

Rapid Rivals

	GMC Syclone	Dodge Li'l Red Truck	Chevy 454 SS
Year	1991	1978–'79	1990–'93
Production	2,995	2,168 (1978), 5,118 (1979)	n/a
Engine	4.3-liter V6	360-cid V8	454-cid V8
Fuel delivery	turbocharger	four-barrel carburetor	four-barrel carburetor
Horsepower	280	225	230-255

Dodge became the first Big Three player to offer a muscle truck after introducing its Custom Sports Special in 1964. Standard for the CSS pickup were bucket seats, racing stripes, and an optional 426-cubic-inch wedge V8. Next came the Li'l Red Truck in 1978, a high-profile half-ton that ranked right up with Detroit's hottest cars that year. Production was 2,168 in 1978 and 5,118 in 1979 (including the model shown here), all equipped with Dodge's 360-cubic-inch, high-performance V8.

Chevrolet got into the performance pickup act in 1990 with its 454 SS. Production of this blacked-out, big-block bad boy continued until 1993, with the final rendition hanging on just long enough to compete with Ford's new SVT Lightning.

GMC's sizzling Syclone appeared in 1991 with all-wheel-drive and a turbocharged V6 that made 280 horsepower. Performance reportedly was a mere 5.3 seconds from 0–60, 14.1 seconds for the quarter-mile.

A hot rod F-150, the Lightning, debuted for 1993 courtesy of Ford's Special Vehicle Team. Temporarily dropped after 1995, the SVT Lightning returned in 1999 with a supercharged V8.

1993–'95 SVT Lightning

Model/bodystyle: F-150 Styleside

Engine: 351-cubic-inch OHV V8 with GT-40 intake, GT-40 heads, and tubular stainless-steel headers

Induction: electronic fuel injection

Compression: 8.8:1

Horsepower: 240 at 4,200 rpm

Transmission: heavy-duty E4OD four-speed automatic

Rear axle: 8.8-inch with 4.10:1 Traction-Lok differential

Brakes: 11.72-inch vented discs, front; 11.02 x 2.25 drums, back

Wheels: 17x8 cast aluminum

Tires: P275/60HR17 Firestone Firehawk GTA

Production: 5,276

Musclecar-like acceleration wasn't the 1993 SVT Lightning's main focus. This hot half-ton also handled unlike any other truck then on the market. Fat Firestone Firehawk rubber on wide 17x8 wheels, heavy-duty stabilizer bars front and rear, gas-charged shocks, and a lowered stance were all part of the package.

According to SVT promotional people, the Lightning pickup was "a Mustang GT with a cargo bed instead of a back-seat." Factory tests produced a 0–60 time of 7.2 seconds. The quarter-mile went by in a bit more than 15 seconds.

GT-40 induction equipment and tubular steel headers helped the 1993 Lightning pickup's 351-cubic-inch V8 make 240 horsepower. Compression was 8.8:1

The original Lightning pickup was built with few notable changes up through 1995. Black and red were the only colors in 1993. A third color, white, was offered in 1994 and 1995. Total production for the three-year run was 11,563.

<u>1999 SVT Lightning</u>
Model/bodystyle: F-150 Flareside
Engine: 5.4-liter (330-cubic-inch) SOHC V8 with aluminum heads and side-exiting dual exhausts
Induction: electronic fuel injection with Eaton supercharger
Compression: 8.4:1
Horsepower: 360 at 4,750 rpm
Transmission: heavy-duty 4R100 four-speed automatic
Rear axle: 9.75-inch Traction Lok w/3.55:1 gears
Brakes: vented discs; 12.1-inch in front, 13.1-inch in back
Wheels: 18x9.5 cast aluminum
Tires: P295/45ZR18 Goodyear Eagle F1-GS
Production: 4,000

A second-generation F-150 Lightning (upper left) joined the action-packed SVT lineup in 1999. Clockwise from top right are the Mustang Cobra convertible, Cobra coupe, and SVT Contour. In 2003, the supercharged Lightning pickup became the world's fastest production pickup, a feat certified by the *Guinness Book of World Records*.

"This is the truck that can run door handle to door handle with a BMW M3," proclaimed a 1999 *Motor Trend* review in reference to the second-generation SVT Lightning.

The reborn Lightning was again available in only three colors in 1999: black, red, and white. Total production that year was 4,000: 1,601 in black, 1,533 in red, and 866 in white.

"The Lightning out performs many sports cars on the road today, and of course it packs all the toughness you expect in a Ford truck."

—*SVT marketing manager Tom Scarpello on the 1999 Lightning F-150*

An Eaton supercharger helped the 1999 Lightning's 5.4-liter SOHC V8 pump out 360 healthy horses and 440 lb-ft of torque. A water-to-air intercooler also was installed.

Medium Graphite cloth (with ebony leather accents) was the only fashion choice inside the 1999 SVT Lightning.

Upper and lower grilles were revised (with horizontal billet bars) in 2001 to help set the 2001 Lightning further apart from its standard F-150 cousin. Exterior clearcoat color choices that year were Bright Red, black, Oxford White, and the new silver metallic.

2001 SVT Lightning

Model/bodystyle: F-150 Flareside

Engine: 5.4-liter (330-cubic-inch) SOHC V8 with aluminum heads and side-exiting dual exhausts

Induction: electronic fuel injection with Eaton supercharger

Compression: 8.4:1

Horsepower: 380 at 4,750 rpm

Transmission: heavy-duty 4R100 four-speed automatic

Rear axle: 9.75-inch Traction-Lok w/3.73:1 gears

Brakes: vented discs; 12.1-inch in front, 13.1-inch in back

Wheels: 18x9.5 cast aluminum

Tires: P295/45ZR18 Goodyear Eagle F1-GS

Production: 6,381

(Left) Twin side-exit exhausts were again standard for the Lightning in 2001. These ceramic-coated tips measured three inches in diameter.

(Below) The name said it all in 2001. Ford's SVT pickup represented an awesome force capable of running from rest to 60 mph in only 5.8 seconds. Quarter-mile performance was 13.9 seconds at 100 mph according to SVT tests.

Restyled five-spoke cast-aluminum wheels appeared for the 2001 Lightning. As before, they measured 9.5 inches wide and 18 inches across. P295/45ZR-18 Goodyear Eagle F1-GS tires went on these painted rims.

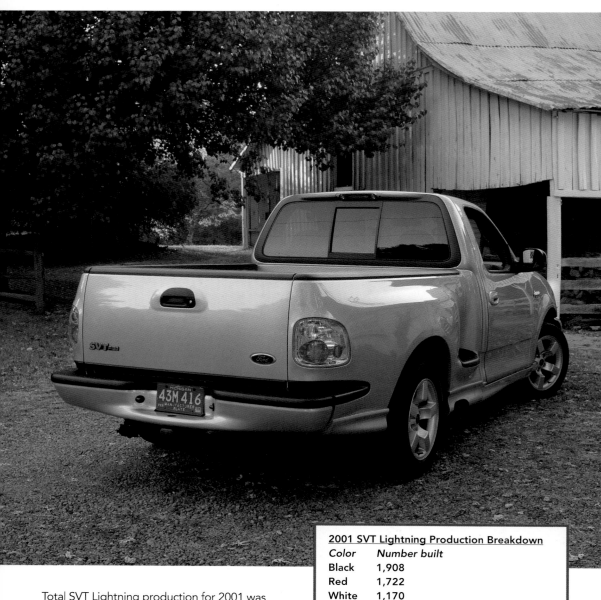

Total SVT Lightning production for 2001 was 6,381. A lowered suspension remained a standard feature. The standard axle ratio was now 3.73:1, compared to the 3.55:1 axle used previously.

2001 SVT Lightning Production Breakdown

Color	Number built
Black	1,908
Red	1,722
White	1,170
Silver	1,581

NOTE: all 6,381 built featured Medium Graphite interiors

Lightning taillight lenses were new for 2001, while a traditional SVT badge once again adorned the tailgate. Side marker lights also were treated to the same clear lenses.

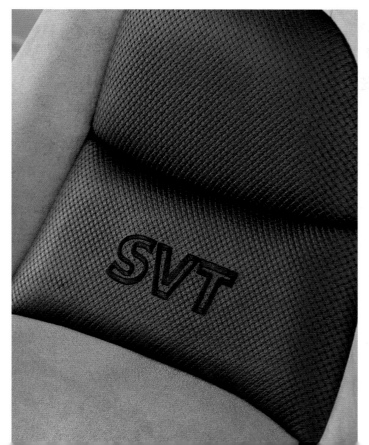

SVT identification typically appeared on the Lightning's 40/60 split-bench seat backs in 2001. Upholstery was a combination of Ebony textured leather and Medium Graphite cloth.

Like its taillights, the 2001 Lightning's head- and fog-lamps up front were covered in clear crystalline lenses marked with faint horizontal lines. The lines reportedly attracted the eye to the lens plane instead of inside the unit to the bulb and reflector.

2001 SVT Lighting Performance		
Road test	0–60	Quarter-mile
Motor Trend, May 2001	6.2 seconds	14.3 seconds at 99.7 mph
Car and Driver, April 2001	5.2 seconds	13.8 seconds at 104 mph

(Above) Lighted vanity mirrors represented the only new addition inside the 2001 SVT Lightning. A premium electronic AM/FM stereo cassette player with a remote six-disc CD changer was standard, as were power windows, mirrors, and locks.

(Left) White-faced gauges, an SVT trademark, were again standard inside the Lightning pickup in 2001. The boost gauge kept track of the eight pounds of pressure supplied by the Eaton supercharger.

Improved breathing characteristics helped the Lightning's 5.4-liter Triton V8 jump up to 380 horsepower in 2001. Enlarged air passages and a bigger 90mm mass-air sensor allowed outside atmosphere a quicker passage into the Eaton blower.

In 2002 the SVT gang showed off a Ranger pickup powered by the Lightning's supercharged 5.4-liter V8. Front suspension components had to be lowered to allow this transformation, and additional modifications included a shortened driveshaft and boxed and braced frame rails. Lightning wheels were used but were widened to 12 inches in back and narrowed to 8 inches in front. SVT called this one-off prototype the Lightning Bolt.

Adding headers and Borla mufflers let a few more ponies loose beneath the Lightning Bolt's Sonic Blue hood. Estimates claimed as much as 420 horsepower for this blown 5.4-liter V8.

<u>2002 Lightning Bolt prototype</u>

Model: Ranger

Engine: 5.4-liter (330-cubic-inch) SOHC V8 with aluminum heads and tubular headers

Induction: electronic fuel injection with Eaton supercharger

Compression: 8.4:1

Horsepower: estimated at about 420

Transmission: heavy-duty 4R100 four-speed automatic

Rear axle: 9.75-inch Traction-Lok (in narrowed housing) w/3.73:1 gears

Brakes: vented discs; 12.1-inch in front, 13.1-inch in back

Wheels: cast-aluminum five-spokes; 18x8 in front, 18x12 in back

Tires: P235/40ZR18 Michelin Pilot in front, P345/35ZR18 Michelin Pilot in back